Blue Jean
Millionaire

Quantity discounts are available on bulk orders.
Contact info@TAGPublishers.com for more information.

TAG Publishing, LLC
2618 S. Lipscomb
Amarillo, TX 79109
www.TAGPublishers.com
Office (806) 373-0114
Fax (806) 373-4004
info@TAGPublishers.com

ISBN: 978-1-934606-34-6

First Edition

Blue Jean
Millionaire

One Man's Insights On Failing Your Way To Success

Charles Whyte

I would like to express my most sincere gratitude to my family for giving me the love, support and encouragement to undertake this project.

Without their help and gentle reminders about stories and events that have occurred through the years, I may have missed much. Not only did they contribute many of the stories, but we had a lot of laughs and walks down memory lane as the process unfolded.

Acknowledgements

I would like to thank Todd Dean for encouraging me to write this book in the first place. If not for that initial suggestion, I may never have started down the path.

I would like to thank Dee Burks and the whole team at TAG Publishing, LLC for their work, effort, patience and especially Dee for the push now and again to get things done. Her insight, suggestions and many conference calls made this all possible.

About the Author

    Charles would describe himself as a completely ordinary guy who is blessed to lead an extraordinary life. Raised in the inner city projects of Toronto, he overcame many destructive habits and mistakes to achieve success. From the dark days of overcoming addiction to financial devastation, he persevered and now enjoys sharing with others how they too can live their dreams. He is very grateful for his family and friends who have supported him and encouraged him to share his message in this book. Charles lives in the Toronto area and enjoys spending time with his five children and many family members.

Contents

Charles Whyte

Chapter 1
Begin at the End

Charles Whyte

Chapter 1

Begin at the End

Many people have had the experience of hitting bottom—of being at the lowest point in their lives when the dark clouds of doom and gloom seem to seep through every part of your life. There have been many times when life has knocked me down or presented what seemed like insurmountable obstacles, but I always got by and things seemed to work out. I rocked along through life, doing what I thought was the best I could do. Still, my life fell apart.

I was 39 years old – fast approaching middle age – and starting all over again. My marriage had fallen apart and the divorce was devastating from both an emotional and financial standpoint. The worst of it was that after seeing and being with my kids every day, they now lived almost an hour away and I only got to see them every other weekend. I moved back to a room at my Dad's house with almost nothing. One of the few possessions I did have was an old car and it finally quit on me, leaving me feeling no better off than when I was as a teen. In fact, I'd had more at the age of 20 than I did now, two decades later. I felt as if I'd wasted twenty years of my life.

I still had a job – but barely. My performance was at best mediocre and the drama of the divorce and my personal problems had taken its toll. My family had suffered the murder of a sister-in-law a few months earlier and then, in the same week another sister in law was killed by a train and my mother died.

I was numb from what seemed to be blow after blow taking its toll on my life and my mind. It's as if I was a hollow shell of a person that barely existed anymore. The week of my mother's death, I sat alone in my room at my Dad's in misery over my life. I was frustrated wondered if it was even worth trying.

I'd tried for twenty years and yet it seemed that everything I'd attempted had failed. The idea crossed my mind that I could just run away from this pit of a life and start over. Obviously, all my old habits and ideas weren't working, so why would I think that I'd ever be successful even if I tried again?

One of the few things I had to keep me company was a cat, who on this day had caught a mouse. The place we lived was nice, but there was the odd mouse on occasion and the cat came in handy for this purpose. That day, as I struggled with what my life had become, I watched the cat play with this mouse.

The cat would lift its paw, allowing the mouse to sneak away and, just before it reached the cold air return to make its escape, the cat would spin around and like lightening recapture the mouse. Then, the game would begin again. The cat would release; the mouse would run; the cat would pounce. It really intrigued me and I have to say I was rooting for the little mouse because it seemed to be trying so hard each time.

After about 15 minutes of this game of catch and release, the cat once again lifted its paw to let the mouse try to escape. But this time, instead of running for freedom, the mouse turned and hopped under the cat. This surprised me – and surprised the cat too! The cat moved away again to give the mouse some room, but once again the mouse ran under the cat. It was as if the mouse had given up and was accepting its fate.

I couldn't help but compare myself to this mouse. Was I really ready to give up trying and just accept this horrible state of affairs? Though it sounds cliché, I had to ask myself, "Am I a man or am I a mouse?"

I got mad at myself because I realized I was wallowing in self-pity. I had my health, people and family who loved me, a job (though just barely), but it was a lot more than some others had. How could I think of just giving up or running away?

Its easy when life is hard and darkness seems everywhere to be overwhelmed by the circumstance—so much so that you lose perspective and discount those things in life that are still good and worth working on. I realized I had to make a conscious decision to put blinders on, shut out the negative events and keep trying. I honestly think if that mouse had given it another shot he'd have made it and I was ready to give it another shot no matter what it took.

That was fifteen years ago. If someone had told me that day that in a short fifteen years I'd be a millionaire, I probably would have laughed so hard I would have cried. But my story isn't unique. A lot of people work hard for ten, twenty, or even thirty years and are then forced to start over. The ones who do well choose to change. The ones who falter or run live in misery. That's not to say the road was easy – it wasn't. In fact, if I'd known how hard it would be, I might have thought twice! But in the end I can absolutely say that decision was the beginning of a journey that changed me for the better and turned me from a mouse into the kind of solid dependable person with a life I'd never thought possible.

When I was young, I wanted to achieve success so that I could be the rock my family depended on. I am now that person. You can completely change your life just by choosing, no matter how difficult the circumstances are right now. No one can do it for you, but if you have the desire, there is also no one that can stop you.

Joe Millionaire

So how does an average Joe become a millionaire? I get asked this question frequently by those who have come to know my life story and I can honestly say that I'm as amazed as anyone at how my life has turned out. I didn't come from money and my parents didn't even know people with money. We were poor and lived in subsidized housing in Ontario during my childhood. My parents never made much money and accepted their lives as they were. I could have done the same and for a time I did – just floated through life taking what came my way but not really striving toward anything.

The one lesson in life I've learned in life is that the only constant is change and life is full of the unexpected. When I was a young man, I thought that my life was going to be a certain way and that I should just accept the hand fate had dealt me. I know now that was a complete misconception on my part. As the world served me a plate full of disappointments, financial setbacks and other hardships, I realized one important fact - I had a choice about how I live and how I respond to challenges and so do you. No one's life is predetermined. When you were born, you didn't have a contract stating how you were going to live pinned to your hospital blanket. You can choose at any moment to accept what life has offered or to choose something different.

Life rarely turns out the way we've planned. I know this has been true in my life. Just like me, I am sure each one of you at one time or another has encountered the unexpected in your life. Content to travel onward in your journey and suddenly, out of nowhere, something blindsides you – maybe an accident, illness, relationship meltdown or a sudden job layoff. There are all kinds of challenges that can swoop into your life at any time and mow down your best laid plans.

These events may be either good or bad, but the fact is that no matter what we must be prepared to handle them. Oftentimes, we sit back and just let things unfold, convinced that if we don't choose a path that things will just work out and somehow stay the same as they always were. But, by not taking control of our fate we are choosing inaction and the consequences for inaction are often much harsher than if we'd made a difficult choice.

Having the benefit from experience, I can look back at my youth and early adulthood and can see where floating through life was extremely destructive. I emulated the behavior and habits I saw around me rather than choosing my own path and it cost me dearly, leaving residual effects that lasted much of my adult life. People who look at me now see a hard working, successful business person and may assume I have no idea what it's like to struggle. Nothing could be further from the truth. I began experimenting with alcohol and drugs at the age of 11 or 12. When I was 13, my younger brother, who was 2 years old, died. It was devastating for me and my entire family and was a real turning point for me as I sank deeper into alcohol and drugs.

I remember as a teen that the father of one of my friends encouraged me, saying I could do anything I wanted. I was smart, got along with people well and had a bright future. His comments stuck in my mind as everyone else who encountered me – teachers, cops, other adults – saw me as a 'bad seed' and on my way to a destructive life. This man had the confidence in me that I didn't have in myself. When you hear others tell you how bad your life or circumstances are, you begin to believe them – even if they aren't completely true. While my life did go off the rails a bit, this man's words would occasionally come back to me and I had the suspicion that he was right from the very beginning.

There are many times that people will see me helping others recover from drugs and alcohol or stopping to give advice to those who seem to be down and out. My view is that I was once in their shoes. Who better to understand than a fellow survivor? I know that no person is unsalvageable or incapable of improving their lives and I take the time to believe in others as someone once believed in me, whether they seem to deserve it or not. I didn't deserve it at the time he offered those words of encouragement yet they have given me something to hold on to no matter how small it may have seemed and helped change my life for the better.

While it may be difficult to understand why certain trials enter your life, I know from experience that there is a definite reason. The challenges you face serve a greater purpose in your life than what you can see right now and there are always beneficial outcomes if you only choose to see them. Often, we experience the most personal growth during these challenging times. In any situation of impasse, conflict or tragedy – when all doors seem closed – it matters that we ask ourselves: what choice can I make in this situation that will improve my situation? How will I choose to live in this moment? I can allow my circumstances to bring me down and live unfulfilled the rest of my life, or decide to rise above my obstacles and prosper. Even when I fail and my choices don't bring about the outcome I so deeply desired, life presents me again and again with tremendous opportunities.

Emotional resiliency is characteristic of all successful people and can be nurtured over time. This gives you the ability to maneuver the twists and turns of the unanticipated and make the necessary decisions to transform your challenges into great achievements. It doesn't matter if you drank yourself to oblivion last night or spent the night in jail. Nor does it matter if you home is going into foreclosure and you have no source of income. You choose how you view each day and what opportunities you will take to improve those circumstances. There's no such thing as hopeless unless you choose to give up hope.

The Enemy Within

I share my story with as many people as I can all in the desire that they can use some of the lessons I've learned. One of the most interesting topics that arises is that many people like to differentiate challenges between those that happen to you and those that you bring on yourself. Those that happen to you are the events in life that you have no control over – where you born, how much money your parents had, and even if you are laid off from a job or become ill and unable to work. Those that you bring on yourself are things such as alcoholism, drug addiction, failed relationships and other items where your actions have direct bearing.

My view is that there is no difference. You choose how to handle every situation in your life – sometimes we just choose poorly. I can honestly say I've experienced almost every positive or negative event that one might have in life

– including the self inflicted type. No one made me pick up that first drink, or the hundredth, I chose. Some may say I emulated what I saw my parents do and that's true to an extent but what I experienced from them was negative – my father took his frustrations out on me physically and my mother mourned the loss of my brother, leading them further into their own alcohol addictions. If anything, this should have convinced me to never take a drink ever – but I chose to. As anyone who has ever recovered from an addiction can tell you, each day is a choice. I choose to be sober, just as years ago, I chose to drink. There is no blame or responsibility laid at the feet of others. I chose poorly; I can change that choice each and every day. I had to work at which included seeking and accepting help and guidance. While it was hard, the freedom from my restraints was worth it.

All this information sounds good in theory, right? But the fact of the matter is that when you put this book down, you may still be facing certain challenges. So what do you do? The first and most important choice for success is to decide that you have the power to remove the obstacles in your life. Many of the obstacles we face in life are internal. Little to no self-esteem, easily shakable confidence, and self sabotaging beliefs about money and what it means, can all hold you back from achieving success.

You have the power to conquer the unexpected by changing your perspective. When you encounter a negative event in your life, face the fact that you've lost something valuable the let it go, rather than dwelling on your circumstance. Refuse to hold onto anger and get rid of any bitterness. It is important to believe in your own success and constantly reminding yourself how bad things are just make them worse. I experienced this type of spiral as a young man when I married at 19, and tried to create the white picket fence kind of life for my new little family. I still struggled with addiction during this time and it was rocky to say the least, but to me it was what I'd always wanted – a real family that was my own to care for and who would care for me.

When the relationship ended, it was devastating, as all I'd worked for seemed to have been wasted. I spent countless hours replaying events and conversations in my head, trying to understand what had happened. It wasn't long until I figured out that this was just keeping me stuck in a rut of failure, making it impossible to move on. It wasn't until I began looking for the good and feeling positive about myself again that eventually led to a life of sobriety and success, but at the time it was very difficult not to wallow in the bad.

A strong belief in yourself and your goals generates these positive emotions. You can choose to make your belief in success become reality. This doesn't mean that you have to be successful before you start, just that you believe you can be successful. It is much like the guy who won't go to the gym until he loses weight so he will look good, but needs to go to the gym in order to lose weight and look good! You don't start thinking about success after you have already made it; you think about it when it's only a dream that you believe in. Believe it will happen.

Live as if you were already successful. No matter what your current circumstances are, imagine them the way you want them to be. Instead of watching TV at home or surfing the web, read inspirational stories of others who have accomplished what you want to accomplish and spend your time with others who are successful. Visualize it as if you were already the multi-millionaire you desire to be. It may seem a little silly to visualize yourself living in a mansion when you are surviving on peanut butter and jelly sandwiches, but the more you picture it in your mind, the more you become convinced that it is possible and that it will happen.

Success is a choice and once you believe in your ability to succeed, you'll soon choose your behavior and actions to accomplish it. Belief is more powerful than most people realize. Don't underestimate it and don't give in to the temptation to ditch those dreams you once had.

We all reach a point where we're sick and tired of our lives. Maybe we feel trapped in a relationship, stuck in a job we hate, or just flat bored and dissatisfied with how things have turned out. What happened to that exciting life you once envisioned? When opportunity lay before us like a huge buffet, ready to be consumed by our eager energy?

The truth is that nothing happened. It's still there – life is still full of boundless opportunity but as we each travel our own path, our vision narrows. We become battered by the storms of life and convince ourselves that those opportunities exist for others, not us. Over time we even cease to believe they exist at all almost as if it were all a confusing mirage. Why do we do this to ourselves? Because it's easy – it is much easier to offer a multitude of reasons why we haven't achieved our dreams than it is to take responsibility for our results. Of course, if you want something better, you're going to have to give up something to get something. You must give up your excuses. I had to.

We all want to be successful, whether that means to be smarter, richer, or more fulfilled. Seems pretty simple, but it's amazing just how many people are afraid of success. Will I be good enough? Will they expect too much? Will they see me as a fraud? Don't be one of those people that allows fear to kill your dreams. You have to want it to get it. I did!

People often think they have to get to the root of the problem before they can solve it. That's not always the case. Some things don't need to be understood; they just need to be dealt with so you can move on. Focusing on solutions is a much more positive approach. The past is over; we've heard that a million times. We still look there and try to make sense of things. Maybe it's because the past is known and the future is not. You have to ask yourself, "where will I find the solutions for my life?" Is it in the past where the results are known and have been dissatisfying or is it in the future where anything is possible? Any lesson learned in life is valuable, but instead of using the past to explain away mistakes, you must use it as a teacher and apply those lessons.

It's You

You are totally responsible for your life – not your family, friends, boss or business interests. This is the foundational principle you must embrace if you plan for happiness and success both emotionally and financially. The most important aspect of taking responsibility for your life is to listen to the little voice in your head. It is a well-known fact that we become what we think about. Blame and excuses are the telling signs of an unsuccessful life.

Have you ever watched a television show where they allow prisoners to explain why they are in jail? You will notice that they have a very predictable and similar pattern in their reasoning and approach to life. Nothing was their fault, including the incidents that landed each of them in jail.

I estimate that if they talked to every incarcerated individual, we would find the same pattern of "not my fault." That is why taking responsibility for choices, actions, and direction is so powerfully important. Without taking responsibility, you'll likely look at your life as a failure because you allowed yourself to be blown in any direction, by any passing wind of circumstance, and then you blamed the wind for how things turned out.

People who take complete responsibility for their lives experience joy and control over circumstances. While no one can control everything that will happen in their lives, we can control our response to any situation and are able to make choices because we understand that we are responsible for those choices. Even when events that are not under your control go awry you can, at least, choose how you will react. You can make an event a disaster or you can use it as an opportunity to learn, to grow, to cherish your faith and to hold loved ones close.

The most important aspect of taking responsibility for your life is to acknowledge that your life is your responsibility. No one can live your life for you. You are in charge. No matter how hard you try to blame others for the events of your life, each event is the result of choices you made and are making. Listen to the little voice in your head and observe yourself talking with coworkers, family members and friends. Do you hear yourself taking responsibility or placing blame?

An important part of changing a negative or blaming thought process is to become aware of it. Many people have a constant stream of negative internal dialogue running through their minds. Just be simply becoming aware, you are able to stop this dialogue and replace it with positive and uplifting dialogue. I discussed this idea with a waitress at a local restaurant a while back as I was dining out with friends. Almost every bit of conversation coming out of her mouth was negative – the state of the economy, the fear of losing jobs, a broken marriage, the problems she'd heard others were having. I talked about how wonderful things were going and what a time of great opportunity we lived in and she was almost speechless. As we discussed this idea of constantly allowing the negative to control your life, she became aware that that was what she'd been doing. She had a great job, wonderful parents, was attractive, with many friends and huge potential. Yet instead of focusing on the good in her life, she focused on the negative that she picked up from people around her.

A short time later I ran into her again at the restaurant and she told me what a difference our talk had made in her attitude. She said it was as if this giant weight had been lifted from her shoulders—and it had. What she hadn't realized is that the weight was completely her own doing and had nothing to do with her life. Just by simply becoming aware, she'd completely changed her outlook. Eliminate the blame, eliminate excuses in your life and focus on the positive. She was willing to take the risk and try again in every area of her life. I have had many personal demons to overcome and at times it seemed unattainable, but with encouragement and support and remaining focused on my goals I overcame them and so can you.

One interesting thing that many people notice when they start to monitor their thoughts is that they suddenly notice how negative the conversations of the people around them are. This can be at home or at work, and frequently its both. When you are immersed in negative whining, complaining, and fearful talk, it can't help but have an effect on you. Again, this is your choice. You can choose to steer the conversation to a more positive tone, or just remove yourself from it if necessary. Eventually those around you will notice your new attitude and start asking how you stay so positive. I can honestly say that my cheerful and positive outlook is one of my most important assets. Now I face each day with optimism and hope rather than dread. I know there are new opportunities that are waiting to be discovered and the challenges I face are temporary.

It's not uncommon for people to perceive that the bad situation they are in will last forever. But change works for you in that respect. Nothing stays the same forever and any situation will improve over time. While your emotions may help you feel desperate or hopeless, the reality is that you are neither – you have time on your side and that means things can and will change. So, when someone offers you advice that can improve your outlook, take it! Just imagine if the waitress at the restaurant had become defensive and upset rather than listening to my feedback on her negative outlook. She would have missed the opportunity to improve her life and lift that heavy weight she'd been carrying off her shoulders. Those that choose to listen and heed the wisdom of others have the best chance to improve in the shortest amount of time.

Happiness is a Choice

Think of someone you know that seems happy about life. How would you describe their attitude? Do you think they are kidding themselves? Are they ignoring the ugly truth about life that's right in front of their eyes and pretending that some happy fantasy world that exists only in their heads is real? Well, guess what? That is exactly how every happy person in the world acts including me. The most interesting thing about individuals that assume happy people have lost touch with reality is that they themselves have actual lost touch, but in a negative way. Reality is, in fact, neither good nor bad—it is whatever you make it to be, meaning that it can be bent and twisted in many directions, depending on your perspective.

You have probably experienced this in your life many times over. Have you ever been in a traffic accident where there were several participants and witnesses? It is amazing how varied the accounts of these people can be. For some, it may have been devastating and frightening beyond reason and, for others, a mere annoyance. Often, you almost wonder if these people were at the same accident at all because their stories are so different. It is not that any of these people are lying or altering the truth. They are recounting their version of reality based on their perspective of the event.

Good and bad, happy and sad, these are notions that you are imposing on the world around you. Happiness doesn't depend on anything that has or has not happened in the past, nor does it depend on your future prospects. The simple fact is, in order to be happy, *you must decide to be happy*.

You can't blame it on anyone else and no one else can do it for you. You've just got to decide to be happy, whether or not your logical mind thinks it is rational to be happy and whether or not your moral sense thinks you deserve to be happy. You absolutely will not be happy for any length of time until you decide to be so and if you decide to be happy, you can continue to be so in the face of even the most miserable circumstances.

The main thing to remember is that you have choices. You don't have to continue to be unhappy or unsuccessful, but our tendency is to keep doing things the same way unless something forces us to start examining those things that aren't helping us move ahead.

Eliminating Barriers to Success

Over the years, I have been very fortunate to help others in eliminating barriers to success in their lives anytime I could. In each situation, I help them discover their own resources and belief in themselves to eliminate any barriers that surface. I have to admit that I have also encountered a few people who can't seem to knock down the barriers. These are the ones who experience fleeting success, if at all, and instead of eliminating barriers, they construct more of them.

The first barrier to success many people point out is a lack of "know-how." You must develop "know-how" or you will not be successful. I can tell you that I haven't gotten to where I am now by spending years in an educational system. Now, I think getting an education is a worthwhile endeavor for anyone, but you don't necessarily have to have a degree to be successful. In fact, some of the highest paid people on the planet never finished college – such as Bill Gates. What is more important is to know that you have to think differently, choose your path and make wise decisions. It's hard work and many people allow themselves to become overwhelmed. They fall back into their old way of thinking and doing things – their comfort zone.

Your comfort zone is the lifestyle that you have become accustomed to. It is where you feel safe and "comfortable." Anyone who has studied physics (or a cow in the road) knows that it takes much more energy to get an object moving than it does to keep it moving. Once I fall into my personal comfort zone, I cease moving. I get used to my surroundings and actively choose not to leave. I sometimes reason that it's better play to it safe rather than step out into the great unknown. It's easy to worry about what other people will think if I risk and fail.

Once we understand that risk is natural, and to risk intelligently is what we are supposed to do to have fulfilling life, we can be more consciously aware of, and ignore, the external forces that will hinder us. It takes a shift in our thought process to create enough desire to move beyond the safety of what we have known.

The next barrier to success is knowing versus doing. Many of us know what to do. We want our time to be our own and to live in freedom. We know we should look for opportunities, take the most promising ones and move forward. If we want different results in our lives, we know we must focus on change. We know that to lose weight, we must eat less and exercise. We know to retire well we must work hard, save our money and create an ongoing income stream. We know what to do – so why don't we do it?

The problem is that we do not change ourselves or our mindset. We focus on the negative by giving in to fear – fear that we will fail and so it becomes self-fulfilling. It is important to repeat that which you think about, you will become.

It is a conscious decision to accept the mindset of a new and abundant life and it takes effort. What people don't realize is that it is easy to make the decision; the hard part is not falling back into the old habits that produced the less than stellar results in the first place.

The power to change any aspect of your life is completely within your control, but only if you change your thoughts. This could also mean changing your associations, but it is necessary if you truly want to live an abundant life. In order to transform your life, and reveal your true self, you must first transform the mind.

The last barrier to success is persistence of action. This is directly linked to the degree of success that you'll realize. Success takes work and the amount of work you are willing to put into achieving your dream is directly proportional to the amount of success you will ultimately experience.

One of the greatest issues we face with this barrier is the persistence portion and I'm no exception. I may start out strong, but then life gets in the way and I put it off and then put it off again. Procrastination is not my friend when I are pursuing my dreams and the same is true for you.

Procrastination, simply stated, is the passive state of frustration when someone can clearly envision a possibility: a business idea perhaps, a career move, or perhaps a house move but all they do is talk about it, think about it, maybe even research it a bit, but then fail to do anything concrete to make it a reality. Action is key! You can't do anything sitting on the couch eating potato chips. If you want it, you have to get up and get it.

One of the most important things you can do to overcome procrastination is to stop daydreaming. A little escape is good for the soul and the imagination is a powerful tool, but there is a line between visualizing your success and just dreaming about it. To do nothing other than dream of future success is actually lazy and ultimately leads to a great deal of confusion. A healthy mind needs to be focused on actually engaging in life. Start to employ your imagination into assessing what needs to be done and whether or not your ideas are worth pursuing, then do it.

Look at your friends and acquaintances and consider how many of them truly have an unshakable belief in where they are headed in life. Would you consider them successful? Whenever a negative thought pops into your mind, train your mind to look for the positive aspect of it. Don't allow worries to stay in your mind long enough to grow into fear. Use your worries as catalysts to begin thinking about your next steps. Keep your focus on solutions instead of on your problems. If you believe that prosperity is destined for everyone but you, ask yourself why. Based on your answer, you may need to change old, unhealthy and/or negative behavior patterns that are preventing you from making the progress you deserve. It's much like exercise; with practice it will become habit.

To some degree, everyone experiences disappointments in life. Difficulties in business, relationships, finances, and life in general are common experiences. At my lowest point, I felt alone and as if no one had ever been in my situation before. You're not alone, so don't isolate yourself. Find other people to talk to and support and encourage each other as you deal with your challenges. Make healthy connections with other people. Notice what people are in your life right now to help and support you. Be grateful for them and listen to their advice and similar experiences. This will help you put your situation in perspective. While you're looking for friends, be a good friend yourself and be willing to help others in any way possible. Those efforts will come back to you and be more rewarding than you ever thought possible.

Learn from your mistakes so you can grow beyond them. Accept your situation and begin to work through it honestly. See the potential that exists. Whenever your old dreams die, there is the potential for new dreams to be born. For this to happen, however, you have to believe in yourself and your abilities. Now, I'm not talking about a half hearted belief; I mean it has to be strong and unwavering, able to withstand any circumstance or situation. If you truly believe in yourself and your ability, something good will come out of even the worst occurrences. Every disappointment can be turned into chance to develop a greater sense of self.

No Excuse to Give Up

Persistence is the refusal to give up, despite whatever delays, backsliding, or setbacks life throws at you. In this section, we're going to talk about how to keep moving toward what you want and away from what no longer serves you. So what will keep you moving forward, you're asking? What's going to separate you from all the other people in the world with the same wonderful intentions of redefining their lives?

You have to ask yourself how many times you can be knocked down and still get up and keep going. What is your limit? Have you given yourself a worst case scenario that will excuse you from trying anymore? Then you are giving yourself a reason to fail. You are hedging your bets rather than giving it one hundred percent and you know what? You're right you will absolutely fail. You can't say I will try it for a year and then I'll let myself give up. You have to give it everything you have and determine in your own mind that there is no going back. Don't give up and let the cat win!

It's easy to only look at the downside of your plans not working out. Instead, explore the new direction this event may take your life. Asses the possibilities you now have. Look for any new avenues for success and walk down them the best you can into your future. Don't worry about getting too far astray; if you honestly believe in yourself, you'll succeed.

Walk confidently in a new direction. Decide to speak positive words that reflect your hope and that encourage others -- no matter how challenging your circumstances are right now. You will always have something positive to offer. Don't listen to advice from negative or bitter people and avoid media content that negatively influences your thinking. Listen to positive people and watch, read, or listen to uplifting shows, books, and seminars. Whenever you're tempted to complain about a situation, remember why you are doing it in the first place and focus on the positive outcome you want to achieve. Gain confidence from placing your trust in yourself instead of in people or circumstances. Be willing to take whatever steps necessary to take you into your future. Although you can't be sure what life will bring, you can be certain that success in inevitable. Believe it will happen.

Throughout this chapter, I've mentioned the choices we have. One of the most important choices we make is discipline. Remember, success is a choice, and it's one that you must make. You can either choose to pursue your dreams and embrace the challenges along the way or live a life where you don't want to get out of bed in the morning. Think about how great your life will be once you make the decision to act. Remember that rich people do what poor people won't. You are in charge of your own life and how it unfolds, not anyone else. You have the power to change and that change can bring the life you've always dreamed of. Why wait?

Chapter 2
One Step Forward

Charles Whyte

Chapter 2
One Step Forward

As many recovery programs teach, the first step is to accept the problem or situation and this is what I did when I made the decision to try again. I was the lowest I'd ever been – I barely had a job, was living with my dad, my children were 60 miles away and I had no car. Things were bad, but I still had options. Once I committed to make the effort to turn things around, the only direction I could go was up. But it was hard—very hard.

I scraped together every last dime I could scrounge up – and even borrowed a little – to get the $700 to buy a car that ran. My goal was transportation, so it didn't really matter what the car looked like. It got me to work and to see my children on the weekend. The bottom of the door was rusted, so I used spray foam to fill in the gaps and then covered it with duct tape. I then used black spray paint to create a stripe on the bottom of the doors so it looked decent. The floor board had holes from rust, so I put a piece of plywood over it and it worked. These were things that I hadn't done since I was a young man just starting out, but they served me well as I struggled to survive.

It's a given that at some point in life we all have to dig ourselves out of a hole of some sort – especially financial. No one is born knowing how to handle money perfectly and even those people who we think are great with money, such as Donald Trump, have also made mistakes that cost them dearly.

Your story is probably not as different from mine or from other people as you might think. Chances are someone's been through something very similar to what you've been through or are going through whether it's addiction, financial hardship, relationship woes or professional struggles. There are even those who have weathered any number of those combined or possibly all of them concurrently as I have. However bad you've had it, there is someone who can relate and help you get through the tough times. But, realize that tough times are never a thing of the past. Life is not static; it comes in waves. There will be times of relative calm and times of intense heartache and these patterns repeat themselves throughout our lives.

In my own life I have, and still do on occasion, experience cycles that are familiar. In my professional life, I would do very well at a job for a few years then rest on my laurels for a while until I was forced financially to once again start excelling. It would seem obvious that if I could produce and make a great income that I would want to do that all the time, but that's not how the mind works. Once we get to a certain level, be it with a job, relationship, or in controlling our own demons, we slip into a comfort zone and put ourselves on autopilot - that's when things start to go off the rails. Think back in your own life. How many times have things been going extremely well at the office, but your home life was a wreck? Or perhaps you were deliriously happy in your relationships only to end up getting yourself fired from work.

Realize that this is part of human nature. When things are going well in one area, we sometimes neglect the other areas of our life. When we are forced to focus on the problem area, we then start to neglect the areas that were going well. Unless you become aware of this cycle, you are destined to repeat it your entire life as this is just normal behavior for the majority of people – it's habit. However, becoming aware gives you the power to change things and achieve that balance you always hear people talk about. Balance isn't sitting on a mountain meditating – it's focusing on each area of your life and understanding how to maximize each one to achieve happiness and contentment instead of chaos and strife.

Normally, breaking any habit and creating new positive habits takes multiple attempts and sometimes those attempts just manage to sink you deeper into your problems. Addiction seems to have a knack for producing these kinds of results and I don't just mean alcohol or drug addiction. Some people are addicted to bad relationships, others are addicted to food and there are many other addictions that can be habitual and hard to eradicate because there is an underlying emotional element. In too many cases, the individual will try to get rid of the addiction – usually on their own first with limited results. At some point they hit bottom and realize there can be no improvement without help dealing with the underlying issues.

But addiction isn't the only area of your life where taking one step forward might result in three steps back. Relationships often have the ability to wound a person beyond anything they ever thought possible. You risk a lot when you open yourself up to a new person who could hurt you, but that's just the beginning. I had the pleasure of knowing a particularly strong woman who had relocated to be with her significant other. Things were going well for her, she felt secure, she enrolled in college in her new state. Two weeks after relocating, her boyfriend cheated on her. She could have returned home to nurse her wounds and allowed this to fester, focusing on the negative event until it kept her from moving forward. Rather than return home crushed and with the added pain of taking the financial hit associated with dropping out of college, she dusted herself off and finished her coursework. Was this easy? No! In fact, she exhibited a wisdom way beyond her years. We often allow these hurts to accumulate and then use them as an excuse for how our life turns out. An excuse is still an excuse no matter how good it seems.

No one's life will be perfect. We will all encounter events where we regret the way we responded, but that's okay because we learn from it. Know that failure is just part of the process and isn't necessarily a bad thing – how else would any of us know what not to do? Failure can, and often will, precede success in any major undertaking in life. That shouldn't discourage you from doing what you know you need to do. Recovering from a bad relationship experience is something you know you have to do because curling up in the fetal position and refusing to move on isn't an acceptable response. The same goes for losing your job or falling on hard financial times – they all require recovery.

It may be true that you experienced particularly hard times through no fault of your own. But explaining that to everyone that will listen isn't going to move you forward. It doesn't matter whose fault it was or what happened. Leave it in the past and accept the responsibility to move forward. Concentrate on what you want to achieve. It takes focused action to set yourself right again and sometimes a great deal of it. At the same time, you also have to set aside the ideas of what this experience says about you as a person and what other people think.

Blue Jean Millionaire

One of the particularly hard areas I encountered that first year as I struggled to get back on my feet was the issue of my children. At the time my daughters were ages 12 and 8 and my son was about 7 years old. I had them every other weekend, but there were often times that I had barely thirty dollars to my name and I knew that gas alone to go pick them up would be $15-$20. I wanted to be a good parent and didn't want them to sit and stare at the walls because there was nothing to do. I refused to give in to the idea that they didn't need to see me or that they might think less of me because of my financial situation, but that meant I had to be creative.

We would often build tents in my dad's basement and borrow a movie from someone to watch together. We also sometimes would build a small fire in an old tire we had in the backyard and enjoy that as a family. One day I was down to my last $10 for the week, so the kids and I went to a yard sale and saw an old used fryer – the kind with a basket to make French fries. It was grungy, but the kids wanted to buy it, so we did. On the way home we picked up a bag of potatoes and some oil. When we got home, we scrubbed that fryer really well, the whole time talking excitedly about how much fun it was to make your own French fries and how good they were going to taste.

You know it's funny now, but my youngest daughter at the time was amazed that French fries were made from potatoes. It's amazing the knowledge that we sometimes take for granted and how an event like this can bring it to light and make it a learning event for children. We spent the rest of the day peeling and cutting the potatoes into fun shapes and then frying them up. At the time it seemed like a small event, but my children remember and talk about it to this day. We really bonded and enjoyed each other's company and that's all that matters in the end, not what I could buy.

This day was priceless. Once I became aware of this fact, I let go of any embarrassment or feelings of inadequacy as a parent and allowed myself to really enjoy my children no matter my financial circumstances.

Prior to this dark time in my life, I often found myself stuck in a damaging cycle in my professional life that you might recognize. I would work hard for stretches getting an investment off the ground, but I would always seem to undo all the hard work I had done by basically giving up on the endeavor.

Once I had worked hard to get things moving, I would coast through the process for a stretch of months until it was absolutely necessary to work hard on the project again. And that's exactly what I did - work hard again. This went on a lot with my professional life in every sector: working hard and coasting, working hard and coasting. It was a never-ending drama that stressed me out and made my home life difficult to bear and this eventually precipitated the drama that led to the lowest point.

Rather than taking the same step forward that I'd taken before and ending up in the same place, I stopped and really thought about who I was and who I wanted to be. I can recall specific moments of frustration with the chaos in my life. I was tired of being seen as the bad seed, the screw up with no future. I wanted to be the solid rock that could be depended on and in my mind that's how I pictured it. I would be the financial rock for my family to come to when they had an emergency or crisis and know that someone cared enough to take care of them. There's nothing worse than knowing those you love desperately need financial help and not being able to do anything about it. So I took the time to decide the person I wanted to be. Then, and only then, could I set out to achieve that.

Creating Your Future

Self-image is how you see yourself in relation to others. This is the idea you have of what kind of person you are which is very important as it affects your self-esteem and confidence level. Self image is made up of a variety of ideas you hold about yourself including how you feel you measure up to others physically and how you perceive that your personality comes across. Self image is revealed by your thoughts and actions. For example, are you self conscious because your teeth aren't perfect? Do you have an engaging personality that attracts people to you? Your self image also includes the kind of person you feel you are: are you honest and abide by the rules or are you ready to do anything to get ahead? All of these items combine with whether or not you like yourself. When you think about yourself, do you feel good or do you feel bad? These emotions have to be dealt with before you can change your behavior.

Self-image is tied very closely to our self worth. Self worth can be described as a personal judgment of worthiness that is expressed in the attitudes we hold about ourselves. The picture we hold of ourselves in our own mind is intimately connected to the value we place on ourselves. Healthy self worth is having a positive constructive view of yourself and your abilities. It allows you to work toward your goals and engage in rewarding relationships. Unhealthy self worth is displayed as a negative, pessimistic or disapproving view of yourself. It is the inability to see beyond limitations and problems. Those who display this type of worth believe that they can't reach goals or have meaningful relationships.

I can say that there have been tremendous shifts in my own self image and self worth throughout my life. As a young person, I didn't have much self worth and my self image was negative. If another hadn't seen a spark of promise and shared that with me I might have lived a very different life. Eventually as I made a home and family, my self-worth and self image grew. But once those things were gone and my life was in shambles, it was very hard for me to feel positive about myself. People often experience this when the negative emotions really take hold and you simply lose hope. That's what I saw when I saw the cat with that mouse. The mouse simply gave up. I had a lot of people who needed me and loved me and giving up seemed very cowardly. It was a long road to rebuild my own self worth and overcome any doubts.

Improving your self-image, like improving any skill, takes time and practice. Developing good self-esteem involves encouraging a positive attitude toward yourself and the world around you and appreciating your worth, while at the same time behaving responsibly towards others. Self-esteem isn't self-absorption—it's self-respect. Now I regularly reflect on my strengths and positive attributes. The only way to improve your ideas about yourself is from within. I always tell people, "It's an inside job."

By working from the inside out and focusing on changing my circumstances, I built back my self-esteem. Circumstances can threaten to drag you down repeatedly, but if you focus on them rather than taking action and doing something to change the situation you will not reach your true potential. It is important to see yourself honestly and accept those talents and good qualities that can help while removing the internal barriers that can keep you from doing your best. There are several small ways to improve your own self-image and confidence and I still use some of these each and every day.

It is important especially when times are tough to avoid the 'all or nothing' thoughts. For example, I could have said,

"I only have $30 this week and my children can't really enjoy themselves for that, so I will stay home." It wasn't reality, but if I had bought into that idea, just think of all that I would have missed! All or nothing thoughts are an exaggeration of reality that you may have even experienced on a daily basis. How many times have you heard or thought, "I always make that mistake" or "I'll never get a good job". These are examples of the all or nothing idea. It's a thought or statement that grossly exaggerates the truth. The real truth is that you can choose to learn from mistakes and you can choose to get a good job if you want one. These negative statements only serve to convince you that it's not possible and are an excuse not to try. No excuse is good enough to give up your dreams.

I talked quite a bit in the last chapter about stopping negative thoughts. I know many people who project their negative thoughts onto others and assume they know what that person is thinking. They may have thoughts such as, "I know they think I'm worthless so why try?" or maybe "They'll never give me a chance." I felt this on occasion when I was worried my children might think less of me because I was poor or that my family would see me as the 'bad seed'. You can never know what someone else is thinking and most of the time they aren't thinking anything close to these assumptions. Even if they were, so what? You can't change the past, but today is an opportunity to give them a new and improved impression of who you are and the kind of person you are striving to be. Today is the first day of the rest of your life!

A good example of this is a man I know named Greg. He was terrible with money, always behind on his bills and borrowing from everyone he knew – most of the time from his sisters. When we talked, I really believed that he had made some tough decisions and wanted to change things

– but he was convinced his family would always see him as a loser and would not give him the time of day. After some encouragement, he committed to work hard and catch up on what he owed. He paid down his debt and became financially stable. Then he went to his sisters and—one by one—paid off the money he'd borrowed over the years. While yes, they were skeptical at first, the fact that he did what he said he would do and proved to them he'd changed made all the difference. Now they are his biggest supporters. Never assume that any situation is beyond repair as long as you are willing to make the hard decisions and follow through. Don't let your assumptions about the opinions of others get in your way. Your actions will speak louder than any words every can.

Whenever I talk to people about focusing on their positive qualities, invariably someone in the crowd will tell me that they just don't have any positive qualities or positive things going on in their lives. This is completely untrue. Each of us has strengths and attributes that are good and make a positive impact on others. It may be the way you greet people, that you are punctual, that you are a great problem solver. I never have claimed to have a perfect life and I don't know anyone else who does, but I do know that by focusing on the good in myself I have made much more progress than I ever might have otherwise.

I have actually argued this point before with a woman who was convinced that you should focus on your weaknesses to make those areas stronger rather than your strengths. I disagree. Focusing on your strengths gives you confidence and allows you to find others who can help you and compliment you in those areas where you aren't as strong. In that way you can learn the skills you need rather than always feeling 'not good enough' because you are focused on your weaknesses.

Having said that, we must all accept our flaws as well and I certainly have my share. But I don't need to dwell on them or make them out to be bigger than they are. If I mess something up or get something wrong, I learn from it and move on. I don't stop and worry about it. Even Warren Buffet gets it wrong on occasion and every misstep is a learning experience. I have known many people who struggle tremendously with what I call the "expectation of perfection". They expect to be able to do everything perfectly the first time. Not only is this completely unrealistic, but it can warp your perspective to convince you that you are worthless when in actuality you are way ahead of the vast majority of people.

A few years ago, I knew a high school girl in the states who was anxiously trying to get into a good college. Half way through her senior year she found out she would graduate fourth in her class. She was devastated! She had convinced herself that unless she graduated first that she would never be able to get into a good school. This expectation completely altered the magnitude of her accomplishment in her own mind. I can't imagine graduating with that high a ranking and yet she was upset. Of course she got into a great school and only then did she realize she'd stressed herself out over nothing. This is true for many people. They are so worried that they won't be the best that they discount how far they've come. Don't let yourself be dragged down by 'shoulda woulda coulda' thoughts. Focus on what you have accomplished and move forward.

The best test for this type of self-bullying, is to notice your thoughts. How would they sound if you were saying them to someone else? Would you tell another person that "You are worthless and can't even get one thing right?" Yet many people run this type of thought through their mind constantly in a kind of mental self mutilation. Or maybe they think "I don't deserve to be happy or have nice things because I've been a disappointment to everyone?" These statements sound just awful when you say them out loud, but many people constantly berate themselves with this type of harsh criticism. Stop it! Rather than criticize your every action, you can evaluate other possibilities. For example, instead of telling yourself, "I didn't make number one and won't ever get there," you might instead think, " I was only a short distance away from the top spot this time – what can I learn to help me improve for the next time?" Not only does this allow you to be kind to yourself, it also acknowledges what you have accomplished and that you can do more if you choose to learn. You must shoot for the stars and even if you land on the moon, that's still an incredible accomplishment.

You are what you think you are. If you think you are smart, resourceful and kind, you will be. If you think you are dumb, sad and worthless, that is exactly what others will perceive you to be as well. I recently came across a simple story that exemplifies this beautifully:

There once was a group of very tiny frogs who arranged a running competition. The goal was to reach the top of a very high tower. As the race began, a big crowd gathered around the tower to watch and cheer on the contestants. No one in the crowd really believed that the tiny frogs would reach the top of the tower. As the race progressed, the tiny frogs heard people talking in the crowd, saying such things as: "There's no way they'll ever make it!" "Tiny frogs just don't have that kind of stamina." One by one, the tiny frogs began collapsing. The crowd continued to talk saying, "See, it is too difficult!!! None of them will make it!" More tiny frogs got tired and gave up—all except for one. This single tiny frog climbed higher and higher. He wouldn't give up and he was the only one who reached the top. All of the other tiny frogs naturally wanted to know how this one frog managed to accomplish such a feat. A contestant asked the tiny frog how he had found the strength to succeed and reach the goal. That was when they discovered that the winning frog was deaf!

The wisdom of this story is that you should never listen to other people's negative or pessimistic ideas. They take your goals and dreams away from you if you allow it. It also illustrates the fact that words have power. Everything you hear and read will affect your actions. I have been helped tremendously by constantly reading positive, uplifting books and learning how to incorporate those ideas into my life. This may work for you as well. You should be positive and, above all, be deaf when people tell you that you cannot fulfill your dreams.

The people in our lives usually do not say things to hurt us intentionally. Very few people choose to be mean, or even thoughtless. Many have so much going on in their own mind they don't realize in the moment how their words will affect others. Remember that it's not what someone else says that matters - it's what you THINK about what they say. I remember how important even the smallest words were to me when I was young. Negative words can have just as great an impact if we let them, so choose to block out the negative and dwell on the positive.

Chapter 3
Your Life is YOUR Life

Charles Whyte

Chapter 3

Your Life is YOUR Life

I've learned a lot about life and a lot about myself as I made the climb from drug addict and alcoholic to millionaire. Thinking back on everything I've picked up through the years, one of the most important things, if not the most important thing that I've learned, is that you can't make excuses. Through all my years of struggle, there was always someone or something to blame for why I wasn't succeeding in life and it would have been easy to place that blame and not accept responsibility for my life.

My parents' habits were passed on to me as I watched them struggle with their own addictions to alcohol. There is a tremendous amount of evidence that an addictive personality and a tendency toward addiction in a parent is frequently and easily passed along to children. I could blame my parents for my hardships, and I did at first. The death of my younger brother had a devastating effect on the entire family and my mother took it particularly hard.

Every family or person has hardships in life – but it is their choice in how they deal with it. As a child, I saw the way my parents struggled with their grief and it was by numbing their pain with substances. There are a lot of people out there who would accept my excuse of tragedy and grief and feel pity for me rather than hold me responsible for my own actions. But I learned that in order to climb out of the pit I created for myself, I had to stop blaming others and stop making excuses and just get to work. This meant I needed a plan.

What you'll find, if you haven't already, is that there is always an excuse available. There is always a reason to avoid doing something that you know needs to be done. There is always a reason to cut a corner. If you don't feel like doing something, there is a perfectly good reason not to do it—you can find it too—believe me, I have. I'm not arguing that point. You may have a very good reason to pass on the opportunity to start your own business or to go that extra mile at work to get ahead but realize it for what it is—an excuse. As I was starting to climb out of the hole, it was not smooth sailing. Times were tough and money was tight. I would often put cardboard in my shoes so they would last a little longer. I know this is not new or unique, but it is part of my journey.

After a year, that old blue car was just really aging. It had been a godsend when I really needed it, but with my 60 mile trips each way to get my kids over the weeks, it was only a matter of time before it had to go. This doesn't mean that I went from the old blue car to a Mercedes—far from it. I picked up an old 4x4 that was in better shape than the car for a little more than I'd paid for the car. My younger brother took that old care and made it work for him for another year (we don't waste!). When we are done with a car we are really done!

The 4x4 was nicer and newer, but far from perfect. In time, I still had to attach duct tape to the door panels and paint them to look good and solid. I patched holes in the floor with cardboard or thin paneling. I used all the little tricks that I had learned, put on a brave face and forged ahead. I didn't get down because others had nicer things; they were just things to me and I had to focus on my goals.

During these tough times I also looked for extra work where ever I could get it. In what little spare time I had, I worked with one of my brothers washing windows. He came to understand that if I said I was coming to work, that I would show up no matter what. This was a definite departure from what most of my family had experienced with me before, but being reliable was one of the things I was determined to be. I also did some painting with a brother-in-law and some roofing with another brother in law. I did what was needed to get by and in the process earned the respect of family and friends and also learned a few new skills. They learned that I was reliable and they could count on me.

If you really want to accomplish great things, then ignore the laundry list of excuses to do the opposite. They are always going to be there and if you give them any credence, you'll always have reason not to act. I like to use the example of starting your own business because it's a somewhat common dream that, while shared by many, is only ever undertaken by a few. If you've ever dreamed of starting your own business, there are plenty of reasons not to. It may be that you're making a comfortable living as an employee at the moment. That's fine, but even in that arena, a little extra effort or creative thinking could improve your income. If you do contemplate your own business, you could be thinking about how you need a lawyer to create a company or an accountant to handle the money and those can be expensive. You might have children to care for and just can't risk having no income, or a variable income, for an undetermined period of time while your business gets going.

They are all legitimate excuses and are likely always going to be there. When one falls by the wayside, it will usually be replaced by another perfectly good excuse to keep going down your same path. In order to break your habits, destructive or not, you have to stop validating your excuses and choose change. You must accept responsibility for where you are in life and choose to make the appropriate changes. Even if you just take the smallest baby step, you have moved forward from where you right now.

The way that I shied away from taking responsibility for my actions and just doing what I knew was right as a young person reminds me of a parable I heard growing up. It's the story of two baby birds dealing with conflicting choices that have led them down two starkly different paths.

Wings of Change

The two birds, we'll call them Charlie and Sam, were brothers growing up in a big city. They lived a happy life and were kept well-fed by their mother. They did everything together, including learning to fly.

One day, their mother went out to hunt for the two and never returned. The two speculated what may have happened to her. Was she killed by a predator? Did she simply fly away, leaving the two to fend for themselves? The two would probably never know, but they did know that they had to take care of themselves because she may never return. The two tried to hunt for and fend for themselves, waiting for their mother to return. Weeks stretched into months and the weather turned from warm and breezy to cold and bitter.

Sam approached Charlie one particularly cold day and said to him, "It's getting so cold that I don't think we can survive here. We'll freeze! I've noticed a lot of other birds flying south, and I think we should do the same."

Charlie responded, "No way, I can't leave my home. I know all the great hunting spots here."

"But winter is coming," Sam insisted.

All of Sam's pleas fell on deaf ears. Charlie had his own excuses for not leaving, which included some good ones – or at least he thought they were good. Sam had tried his best to convince Charlie to fly south with him, but finally decided he had waited long enough and flew south by himself.

Charlie sat in his nest alone and thought about how awful his situation was. The cold was really starting to set in and he was all alone now without his mother or brother to help him survive.

"How could Sam expect me to uproot myself like that? Flying south is such a long trip, and I'm still dealing with my missing mother," Charlie grumbled.

Sam eventually made it south and stayed warm and healthy all through the winter months. Meanwhile, Charlie had to deal with freezing winter storms while trying to find worms in the snow-covered and oftentimes frozen ground.

Charlie held on as long as he could as it became increasingly obvious that he made the wrong decision. He got weaker as he found less and less food to sustain him. As the winter grew colder, Charlie continued to weaken until he froze to death one night trying to find food.

Sam had changed to accommodate the situations that presented themselves and to meet his goal of survival, while Charlie was unbending and allowed his past hardships to act as excuses to wallow in self pity. At the end of the winter, Sam was healthy and happy while Charlie paid for choosing to dwell on the past and live within his comfort zone.

Charlie and Sam can teach us a very valuable lesson about our life choices. We are presented with choices all the time that allow us to step outside of our comfort zone, to stop thinking about how hard our situation is and stop letting the negative events in our lives force us into uncomfortable or downright dangerous situations. We stand to learn much more by putting our fears aside and doing whatever it is that we want to do with our lives. By not letting past experiences dictate our actions, we free ourselves from those burdens. I learned from the negative events in my past and started to work on developing better work habits that would make me more valuable to the company I worked for and it showed.

I'm not saying that you shouldn't learn from your mistakes, but sometimes bad things happen through no fault of our own. Sometimes life is just hard and there is no lesson to be learned or action that you need to change in response to it. It's just that every once in a while, you are dealt a bad hand. Those that play their bad hand and lose don't have to give up or allow it to haunt them. They can choose to move past the error in judgment and regain control of their lives. I made mistakes and had what some would consider failures. They were real learning experiences for me. I kept an open mind and when a new opportunity came along, I was willing to investigate it and possibly participate. When you have a failure or make a series of mistakes it can be easy to shut down and refuse to allow yourself to take risk. But that doesn't serve you well in the long run.

There is no doubt that we are often the source of our own pain because we react poorly to circumstances. If Charlie had realized that he had made the wrong decision, he could have flown south for the winter and continued his life. He had made the wrong move, but never took responsibility for it and never made the necessary changes to correct his mistake. Even as the winter grew colder and it became more and more obvious that things were not improving, Charlie remained steadfast and stubborn. He refused to acknowledge his mistake and stayed the course. We must be persistent, but willing to change if needed.

You have to make the difficult decision to accept the fact that you have made mistakes – we all have - and it's up to you to choose to acknowledge those errors and then choose a better path. This personal responsibility is a learned behavior, so don't feel as though it's too late or not something you can do. With a little practice and concerted effort, you can and will make the necessary changes. It is never too late – I know it wasn't for me, but when I sat watching the cat play with that mouse I thought it might be. I was pushing forty and not only starting over—starting over with a lot of strikes against me. I proved that I could overcome, but I didn't necessarily have the confidence that it would turn out so well back then. You can't let yourself get trapped into thinking something is hopeless. There are always options if you are willing to look for them.

It is never easy to say, "It's my fault." But the truth is that it often is your fault and the quicker you are able to admit that, the sooner you can move past your mistake and set things right. Sometimes we like to point a finger at someone else because that culpability weighs so heavily on us that we can't bear to take the blame by ourselves.

There is shame tied to our wrong moves, but it isn't necessary to punish yourself for making honest mistakes. We pass the buck in an attempt to assuage our pride and our ego. To blame someone else lets us off the hook so that we can continue what we're doing without any feeling of guilt. But when we mess up and don't allow ourselves to acknowledge it, then we'll never fix it.

I learned a long time ago the value of a quick apology or an immediate admission when I made a mistake. I found out that when I am responsible, delaying the inevitable admission makes things that much worse. By addressing the issue quickly, it allows everyone, including me, to move on immediately instead of having to wallow in the dread of knowing I made a mistake.

Even if I'm not sure I'm to blame, I will try to take responsibility. This is due to the fact that I have found that an admission on my part allows others to admit their part in error as well and we can all start anew. Playing the 'blame game' works just the opposite. I blame you, you blame me, we both blame the powers that be and no one gets anywhere!

By blaming others, we lie to ourselves and we tell ourselves that it's others who are making the errors and need to be set straight which puts us in limbo. But the world can't be at fault for everything that goes on in my life or yours. The world is not going to change so that we can stop struggling through life, with alcoholism, addiction, a dead-end job, or financial pressure, or whatever else we may struggle with. All of us have to adapt to our surroundings, not the other way around. Just like with the birds, winter was not going to go away just because Charlie couldn't admit his error.

We have to choose the difficult path and change our own actions and behaviors in order to get on the right path. It is important to change any knee-jerk reactions to put the blame on someone else, on society, on our parents or whomever. Telling yourself that everyone needs to change but you is an illusion and, sorry to say, it's never going to happen. You can wait for it forever or you can choose to change your own behavior.

When I divorced and my children lived in another town, I could have been angry and made things difficult for everyone involved. Instead, I accepted responsibility for my part in the situation and focused on how I could spend time with my children and support them as a father. There were many things we shared during those times which created great memories for all of us and those are things I might have missed had I chosen to blame others. Things aren't always about you and I understood that while I was struggling. I had to look outside myself for opportunities to improve my life and my relationships.

During this time of hardship in my life, I was presented an opportunity to join a multi-level marketing company. I know many people who are successful at this type of business and I also know vast numbers who are not. The person who presented the idea was a friend and I signed up to help him out more than anything. Though I didn't do much with it at first, after a few months I decided to take it seriously and work it as a business.

Slowly, I started to have some success. It wasn't fast or instant and it took a lot of work, but I committed myself to change and this was part of that change. My kids even helped out when they were with me. It is okay to let people help you – including your children and family – when you need it. Quite honestly, there were times when I was living in my dad's basement that my children or myself might have gone hungry if not for his well-stocked refrigerator or my sisters open invitation to meals. I knew one day that I would be the one they could depend on and that has definitely been the case, but I wouldn't have made it without their help. There is no shame in allowing those who love you to help get you on your feet. They are your support system and you will soon be able to be their support system too.

Choose Because It's Hard

In the '60's, John F. Kennedy, President of the United States, set a goal to put a man on the moon in a decade. He gave a speech that stated that they choose that goal, not because it was easy, but because it was hard. They achieved that goal. All worthy goals are by their very nature hard. They require strength of character and determination to accomplish. If they were easy, everyone would have great accomplishments, but they don't. You have the power to choose the hard, but vastly more rewarding, road.

It's never too late in life to change. You can admit failures or weaknesses and set things straight at any point. It doesn't matter if you are 8 years old or 80 years old. No one's actions are responsible for your place in life, so stop excusing your inaction. It's possible to change direction at any point in your life. Take, for example, senior citizens who enroll in college courses or those over forty who are writing their first book. Saying that it's too late to change course is like saying that it's too late to be happy or that it's too late to live a better life. It truly is never too late.

You are the solution to almost any problem you may have in your life. If you have a money problem, you can solve that. If you have an addiction problem, you can recover – but you must choose to do so and then do the work. Very few people realize the real power they have to alter, control and completely change their life and their circumstances. Find your reason and then choose to change.

I recently heard of a young teacher from New Jersey who, in the early 1990's, desperately wanted to travel to Europe – Italy in particular. Her family wasn't wealthy and didn't travel much, but she was determined to find a way to go. After two years of telling everyone she met about her dream, she ran across a teacher from England who'd come over to the States through a teacher exchange program. After some investigation, she discovered that the same type of program was available in Italy. It took another 18 months, but she was finally able to go live in Italy for a year.

She didn't let the reality of her present situation to stop her from dreaming or convince her that she couldn't change things. Consequently, she found a way and it happened. She met a history professor while she was there and three years later they were married. She now lives happily with her husband and two children in a little historic town in Tuscany.

It will probably be a tough transition from someone who consistently takes the wrong road to get headed in the right direction, but it can be done. Many people claim that it takes 21 days to change or establish an act as a habit. Making the right decisions until they become habit is one way of changing your behavior for good. For those of you that can't just dive right into a total change in direction from your former ways, a slower, more thoughtful way of changing things may be in order. Baby steps work just as well as cataclysmic changes, so don't think you can't start right now today with one small change.

Consider the circumstances of your path. Circumstances are probably the reason you don't change your ways from damaging to productive. If you find yourself making excuses for why you can't or shouldn't change direction in life, then you are using your circumstances to bail you out of what you know needs to be done. "I can't start a business right now because..." "We can't afford to take that dream vacation because..." People who utter these phrases, or phrases like them, are using their circumstances to convince themselves that it's just too hard.

People who truly want to make that change do it regardless of whether or not they have enough in savings or have the free time. When you really want something but don't have the funds, "focus on the possibilities" rather than the problems. That's what people who make things happen often do. They know that the money will be there when they need it. They act and have faith in themselves to put everything in order. It was scary, but it's what I needed to do.

People who feel stressed and overworked aren't likely to go start their own business even if they want to. That's because they don't have enough time and energy to what they love when they get home from work and handle the necessities of family life. But those who truly have a passion for owning their own business will set aside some time to start building it on the side in addition to doing what needs to be done to support their families.

I started my business in addition to working full-time. Yes it was hard sometimes. There were choices and sacrifices I had to make with my time, as well as with my money. Would it have been easier to do nothing? Absolutely! But I had goals I wanted to reach. I wanted to be financially stable and provide for my family. I envisioned a cottage on the lake for us to enjoy our time together and all of those goals have happened because I refused to do what was easy. I even collected pop bottles to turn in and make money. But I didn't lose sight of the fact that I could work hard, scrimp and save and do whatever so when a windfall like pop bottles or cans or beer bottles came my way I would put just a little aside to treat myself and my kids. Even the little rewards or treats can make the journey more enjoyable and your resolve even stronger. I was never ashamed to do honest work to make a buck and that helped me reach my goals. Looking back, it wasn't nearly as hard as I thought it would be and I could look at myself in the mirror and be proud.

If you continue to make excuses, then you have to begin wondering if you actually want it in the first place. Everything will come in time. The money will be in your account when you need it. You will have the time to make it all work. Have faith in yourself to make it happen.

Changes like this to your decision-making process are vital to directing your life into a new course of action. Not only will this thought process allow you to do things that you've always dreamed of doing, but taking control of your life instead of just dealing with what happens gives you a much more positive outlook. Self-doubt that many people carry around with them can be crippling and lead down unhappy yet familiar trails to dissatisfaction and even addiction.

It's also important that your faith in your own abilities be unwavering. That can be a lot to ask of someone who is trying to change for the better and is stepping into unfamiliar territory. It's also one of the very reasons I try so hard to encourage people when I can. A friend's father gave me some vital words of encouragement when I needed them as an angry and struggling teen and I want to be that support for others. Confidence can be fragile at first as someone sets out on a new path, especially if it's something they have attempted before without success. Many addicts feel this gripping fear of failure – long before they try to get clean. They know it will be hard and they also know that there is a huge potential for relapse. But many others experience this same fear in other areas of their lives. How many people do you know give up on relationships because they've tried and failed a few times. I've been down that road myself and it's very difficult to try again when you've had devastating failure. I felt strongly about this and yet I forced myself to try once again. Today I am happy because I allowed myself to try again (nothing ventured, nothing gained).

The same is true in finances. If you have perhaps tried to start a small side business before and it didn't work, it can be very discouraging to think about trying again. But, then, as we all know the people who achieve their dreams didn't do it by getting it perfect the first time. They tried over and over again until they found a way. You have to commit to the process because it is a process, not a one shot miracle.

We are Addicts of the Comfort Zone

The person who dips their toe in the water and turns away is someone who didn't really try at all. The only failure is to not really try. You are striving toward your dreams and nothing should ever stand in your way – certainly not your own fears!

If you think striving to be a millionaire, or achieving your goals is too farfetched, then that's like saying your dreams aren't worthy of your effort. I can tell you that if an addict can become a millionaire, then so can you – the only question is do you want to? Before you answer really think about the question – do you really want to?

Now that may seem like a ridiculous question because who would say no? But many people do. They don't say no to wanting more money; they say no to the effort it takes to do so. They say it's not worth it because they would have to risk failure, be uncomfortable and stay focused – and it's easier just to keep going in the status quo. Why is it that you rarely see someone in the early stages of addiction seek help? Because they are reasoning with themselves and making excuses. They are convincing themselves that it's not necessary, or its too much trouble. They can keep going on the status quo. Rich people do what poor people won't and if that means collecting pop bottles or cans for cash, then so be it.

We are all addicted to our own comfort zones, even if you've never touched drugs or alcohol in your life. You are still addicted to the habits that keep your life within the bounds you've become accustomed to. This means you are used to making a certain amount of money, going to particular places and keeping in contact with a specified group of people. Can that change? Absolutely, but not without your concentrated effort. Just like an addict going to rehab, you must focus intently on those things you wish to change or risk relapsing into your old habits and patterns of behavior. I consciously made new habits. I practiced those habits and then practiced some more until they were imbedded in who I was as a person.

You've probably heard before that you don't fail until you no longer try. Think of an inventor, like Thomas Edison, and how many times they must fail before they finally succeed and build that functional prototype. It is estimated he failed 10,000 times before producing the first workable prototype of the incandescent bulb. Many people would look at that scenario and think, "He was nuts! I'd never try 10,000 times!" Why not? You can't strive toward a goal and say, I'll give it one try, or five trys or even 5,000 trys. To do this is to limit your success right up front and thus almost guarantee that you will fail. There can be no limit until the goal is reached and when you decide that nothing will stop you, you will succeed.

I know many times I would look at a happy couple or wealthy person and think, "I want to be rich or happy" like they appeared to be. But I had no idea how many times they tried before they got to that point. Now I know the answer: they tried as many times as it took! Today, I try as many times as it takes. It doesn't matter how many failures there are as long as you keep trying to get that one success.

Choice and Change

We all can look back on events in our lives and easily see those moments when we had the opportunity to choose the direction of our lives. The funny thing is that these important moments in your life can really sneak up on you when you are the least prepared to make some sort of profound decision. It's not like the climax of a movie where everything led to this pivotal point that requires you to make a hugely important decision and you're well prepared and ready. Sometimes they are waiting for you when you wake up one Saturday morning and suddenly have the decision plopped in your lap like a stack of bad pancakes. They come unannounced and without any fanfare. And the fact that they can come camouflaged as a mundane moment in your daily routine makes them all the more difficult.

I know all too well that these kinds of choices can creep up on you like a tiptoeing child to present you with a seemingly innocent question – do you want to take path A or B? Sometimes you don't even think twice and choose from those habitual thought patterns, not even realizing you had the power to change and take a new direction. There were many doors I left unopened because I didn't even notice them or habitually chose an alternate route that was much less beneficial.

The awareness that you have the ability to choose and the strength of will to make the hard choices, determines the life you will lead. Be aware of your situation, your options and what they all mean and make an effort to choose the one that will have the most positive results for you. That may not mean the best short-term results. Quitting your job to start your own company may have a drastic negative effect on your income – but hopefully that's only temporary. Giving up your free time to stay up late and work on freelance projects may mean you are more tired or grumpy, but again it's temporary. And if it gives you the confidence to quit your day job and do what you truly love, then it is very valuable in the long run.

This doesn't mean you have to start your own company; that is just one of the paths I took. But it does mean seeking out your true purpose in life and doing what you love instead of punching a clock. If you already love what you do, how you can make yourself more valuable to that company? How can you help others? There are many ways to fulfillment and success depending on how you personally define them so allow yourself the chance to dream and figure out what it is that really motivates you.

Then understand that no amount of motivation and planning will change your life's circumstances. Only when that motivation translates to action do you have a chance to accomplish your goals. This is your chance. Now. Today. This moment. Will you take it?

Charles Whyte

Chapter 4
Underestimated and Underrated

Charles Whyte

Chapter 4
Underestimated and Underrated

We all live in a world where expectations are small and goals very limited. Rarely are we encouraged to do our best or strive to achieve more. The voices of gloom and doom can convince anyone that it's almost ridiculous to even try to achieve more than we already know or already have. This is one of the most insidious and damaging attitudes human beings can ever experience as negative reinforcement has a tremendous effect over time.

I saw this in my own life in most of those around me as I was growing up viewed me as a trouble maker and predicted that I would only decline in capability and accomplishment as I aged. When these types of assumptions are put upon a young person, that person has very little ability to fight off those feelings of inadequacy and often this becomes a self-fulfilling prophecy. The little encouragement I did get from others made a tremendous impact and stood out to me, giving me something to cling to when things didn't go as well as they could have and often didn't.

There was a time when I first started the journey back uphill, when I held a weekly business opportunity meeting in a major hotel with some other like-minded people. My responsibility was to book the meeting room and pay for it. At this time, I had 2 Visa cards and on any given week, one or the other would be declined. I spent many anxious moments with Visa on the phone convincing them to cover the amount. We would collect a minimum amount of money at the door of the event to help cover the cost of the room. Many nights the take from the door would not cover the amount I had put on my Visa. I would take most of it and put it back on my Visa, keeping about $10 to buy some milk and bread as I was otherwise broke.

During this time, I often felt defeated and allowed my own negative thoughts to enter. Self-doubt can be hard to battle, but battle it I did. I know that I have no control over what thoughts enter my mind, but a lot of control over how long I entertain those thoughts. If I listen, even to my own negative thoughts, then I'm not being the 'deaf' frog that I should be. I have had many periods where I had to juggle bills and expenses, robbing Peter to pay Paul, but keeping my ultimate goals in mind helped me to remain steadfast.

When I listen to the pessimistic and negative views of others, they have a tendency to bring me down and this may be true of you too. Those views can take our dreams and goals and tie them down so that they can never be realized. The people that really want to get ahead and to accomplish whatever it is that they set out to do will find things come much easier when they don't listen to those people out there who are ready with reasons why you will never get it done. Be headstrong and positive and you will increase your chances of making your dreams a reality.

I also heard the story of a college professor who taught physics. He listed some problems on the board and then explained that each was progressively harder, culminating in a problem that had stumped scientists for years and still remained unsolved. He told the class to work through as many problems as possible so he could gage where they were in their learning. As the assignments were handed in the next day, only one of the students handed in the assignment with all the problems completed – even the last one that had been thought to be unsolvable! The most astounding fact was that they student's work was correct. He'd solved one of the most difficult equations known. When asked how he did it, he replied that he'd been late to class the day before and hadn't heard the professor's instructions, so he thought that they had to solve them all – and he did.

This story also helps us realize that what people say has an impact on our perspective before we even try. Words have power. Words can drag us down if they're negative and keep us from realizing our full potential. When you set out to do something difficult that you aren't sure you can accomplish, what you need is encouragement and support. This will help you gain that self confidence that you can accomplish your goals. But when we receive the opposite, we often find ourselves struggling and thinking in the back of our mind that maybe that person was right – we can't pull this off.

Unfortunately, I've been there. I know what it's like to be surrounded by friends and others who doubt your abilities to do even the simplest things like get back on your feet and earn a living. It's not only that you feel bad about your situation, but everyone else constantly reminds you how bad it is and only makes it worse! I've faced these issues myself and know just how damaging they can be. What I've learned is that you have to defend yourself from the negative thinkers in your life. You have to be deaf to them just as the frog in the story was deaf to all the negative chatter about the likelihood of him finishing the race. When you learn to put the proverbial blinders on to all of those around you that think, and say, you will fail, you'll take an important step toward realizing your dreams.

The Chip On Your Shoulder

Not only can you shut out the negativity in your life so it doesn't affect you, you can also use that negativity as a motivating factor. Maybe that negative voice is the voice of a mentor, parent or friend in your life whose opinion you value but who doesn't see that you can really accomplish a particular goal. You have the opportunity to win them over by proving what you can do and their negative opinion may be just the motivation you need. This has occurred many times in my life, whether I had career problems, financial problems or even relationship problems. I used the negative circumstances to pull myself up off the couch and really perform because I had something to prove. I'll show them!

I'm reminded of fellow Canadian Steve Nash, a professional basketball player in the NBA. After many successful years with the Dallas Mavericks, two of which included trips to the league's all-star games, Nash's contract expired and he found himself in an unexpected situation.

The Dallas Mavericks front office took into account Nash's age and injury history, and, based on this, seemed to only half heartedly pursue a contract extension with the star.

Nash, undoubtedly feeling like a major contributor to a club that had turned from bottom dweller to elite team, was expecting a healthy offer to re-up with the Mavs. What he got instead was a lowball offer and a feeling that the team preferred a different point guard and was willing to let the former all-star sign with a different team. Shortly after, the Phoenix Suns extended a healthier offer to Nash that was more in line with what he was expecting.

Nash, out of loyalty to Dallas and its fans, allowed the Mavs the opportunity to match the competing offer and pay what was obviously his fair market value of approximately $10 million per year. The Mavs owner, despite being known as a billionaire spendthrift, passed on the opportunity to match the contract and keep Nash on his team. Nash signed with the Phoenix team that offered him a contract and immediately produced two trips to the conference finals for the club, just one series win away from the league championship, while gathering consecutive league Most Valuable Player awards. All this despite Nash's advanced NBA age (early 30's) and problematic back.

Many fans of the Phoenix Suns would tell you that Steve played with a chip on his shoulder for those two seasons and even beyond. They would claim that Nash felt slighted by the Mavs personnel and played at a higher level than anyone thought possible. They would tell you that there was an obvious vendetta, that Nash felt as though he was insulted and that he played like a man possessed. His work ethic and competitiveness was unmatched by anyone in the league. That's why it's no surprise to me to read in the news today that Nash has signed yet another contract with the Phoenix Suns that will pay him north of $30 million over the next three years – almost until Nash reaches his 40's.

"This is incredible for a player of his age to merit this kind of contract," said Nash's agent, Bill Duffy in a news article following the contract extension. "It's an absolute tribute to his greatness."

Steve Nash exemplified what it is to take a negative comment or feeling – whether real or imagined – and turn it into something that makes you better and helps you accomplish possibly even more than you set out to. The team owner in Dallas thought Nash could very well sit out large portions of a new contract with injuries being in his early- to mid-30's, but instead Nash was earning MVP awards and playing better basketball than he had ever played in his life at a time when his career should have been on the downturn. And, now, when Nash should consider himself lucky to get a contract with any team in the league, he has signed an extension for more than $10 million per year that will pay him until he's 38.

What I like so much about Steve's story is not just his ability to turn a perceived insult into a reason to try that much harder, but the fact that he was able to do it at a time that conventional thought would have him in the twilight of his career.

It's a testament to the power *you* have over your actions and over how you let things affect you. I know that after the last round of divorce and financial hardships I was facing, it was easy to listen to the few detractors and the little voice in my head that said, "I just can't do this again." But, then I let myself get just a little angry at myself because I know I have to do what it takes, as many times as it takes, until success is mine. I decided that I would show them! And I would show me at the same time! You can choose to crumble in the face of criticism or it can be that chip on your shoulder that pushes you to be better. In my case, it pushed me on and kept me asking, "Am I a man or a mouse?"

Choose Happiness

When I am criticized or told that I can't do something because I don't have it in me, I do everything I can to put those hurt feelings aside. Hurt feelings aren't going to get me anywhere in my attempts to stay on the right path. You have to make a conscious effort to see those criticisms as what you have to overcome. They can be a driving force behind doing whatever it is you want to do. This is effectively turning yourself into one of the few optimists. And it's optimists who typically accomplish the most. My glass is always ½ full not ½ empty and it's a choice for me to view life that way. This has been, and I hope always will be, the way I choose to look at life. It has gotten me through many hard times and has been a struggle to maintain sometimes because of the little voice of doubt. But every time I waver, I shake my head, remember the glass is ½ full, and then I feel better almost instantly because I know things are never as bleak as they appear. There is always a solution if I look hard enough.

If you're the sensitive type, and don't be ashamed if you are, then allow yourself a little time to wince after a particularly rough criticism. Sometimes those harsh words can mean more if they come from a particular respected source or if there is some truth to them. Those baseless insults are easy to discount, but it can really smart when someone you care for and respect doesn't believe that you can accomplish your goal. We'd all like to instantly be over that biting criticism the moment it hits our ears, but that's just not how a lot of us operate, me included. We need at least a little time to adjust to the idea that someone close to us doesn't believe in us. Remember that it's okay; not everyone is going to believe in us all the time, but I need to believe in me all the time and so do you. I have to always be my #1 cheerleader,"go team Charles go!!'"

I will tell you that I had to learn to believe in myself – it wasn't a natural instinct when I was young. As my life deteriorated and disintegrated around me, I came to the point where I had to make a strong choice. Would I continue on, or would I make the change? There was a man at that time who believed in me much more than I believed in myself. He encouraged me to keep going and gave me the support I needed until I really started to believe that I could change.

It's important to note that when I made the decision to change my life, I did it for the wrong reasons. My wife was on the verge of leaving me. Our first child was on the way and she bluntly said that she didn't want to raise a child with the kind of person I was at the time. This was the catalyst for me – not my own desire to actually change. But the positive experience that I gained even in those first weeks and months showed me a life that could be very different. As I'm writing this chapter, I am also celebrating the thirty year anniversary of that decision. Yes, in some ways it seems like just yesterday, but in reality I've lived an entire lifetime since then. My children never met the man I used to be and I'm grateful. Because of my persistence and desire to stick to the plan, we have had many incredible times together and I actually have great memories of those times because I didn't ruin whatever event we were at because of my attitude or addiction. I'm also amazed that change actually lasted! I truly like the person I have become and I believe others do as well.

If you're able to focus on what you want, then you have chosen happiness. Choosing happiness means simply seeing the positive in situations and having the commitment to follow through. If you've ever seen one of those eternally happy people and thought to yourself that they've lost touch with reality, they haven't. They are simply choosing to see the positive.

Reality is neither good nor bad. Your perception of it is what makes it what it is. You can choose to make it something that forces you into tough decisions that stress you to the point that you are physically unhealthy. Or you can choose to see those issues as challenges you are eager to overcome. It doesn't change what is, but merely changes the glass you are choosing to see life through.

I'm reminded of a friend who had a car accident on his way to work one morning. He was traveling alone on an icy stretch of highway when he lost control of the vehicle and spun into a ditch. In part because there was no damage to the vehicle and no injuries to himself, he recounted the story happily and with a great sense of relief. Rather than being upset about the accident, he chose to view it as a close call and was thrilled that it turned out well.

Others in that situation may have been frightened to the point that they were reluctant to drive on ice again – which is a big issue if you live in Canada! They might choose to recount the story in a shaky, emotionally distraught manner and allow it to complicate their lives unnecessarily. And there are many that would completely understand this emotional state and do what they could to help – thus enabling the negative emotions to continue. They could offer to be a chauffeur until the friend is comfortable driving again, provide emotional support and be there in any way they could. But why choose that outcome for yourself when you can view your accident in a much more positive and healthy way? If I look at something in a positive way, it almost always works out better than if I view it negatively. Besides, nothing was damaged and no one was hurt. Aside from that, accidents are going to happen – especially when driving on ice.

You can choose to see the negative and let it devastate you to the point that you are too scared to drive and even become burdensome to friends and family or you can see that something happened that was statistically bound to happen sooner or later and that it turned out fine. It's also true that once it finally happens, the chances of it happening a second time are statically reduced. There are healthy ways to view just about everything that happens in your life, but choosing how to view them is entirely up to you.

Breaking Free

Allowing a few negative words to keep us from owning our own business or fulfilling our potential puts you in a box that you can never escape from – but the limitation is only in your mind; it's not reality. The way this happens is through reinforcement of that same idea repeatedly—much like the way elephants are trained to stay put.

When an elephant is born into captivity, it can be tied to a stake that is hammered into the ground only a few inches. Being that the calf is so young, small and weak, it doesn't matter how much it wrestles to pull the stake from the ground and win its freedom, it just can't do it. The calf continues this exercise fruitlessly for a while in its youth until it becomes convinced that the stake is an immovable object.

By the time the calf has gained more than enough size and strength to pull the stake from the ground, it has already learned that its attempts to do so are useless – so it doesn't even try. That's why, if you've ever gone to the circus, you see ten-ton elephants kept in place by a rope and a piece of plastic hammered 5 inches into the dirt. It's so small, so insignificant, yet it is able to keep the elephant under control – not because the animal is restrained, but because it has been *convinced* that it is restrained. A biting comment or criticism can have much the same affect on us in our everyday lives restraining us from developing our true potential. I noticed that the mouse was trained to accept its fate in a much shorter time.

We sometimes allow comments and criticisms of maybe no more than a handful of people keep us from doing what we want with our lives. They've maybe hammered these beliefs into us so that those one or two comments, whether they're true or not, hold us back and keep us from breaking out of the box. They hold us in place and keep us in our normal and possibly unhealthy routine. You, just like the elephant, may not even be attempting to accomplish your goals because you've learned, or more accurately, you've been convinced, that you can't do it.

It's cliché, but the power of positive thinking really can change your life. In fact, it's one of the most powerful strategies one can employ to accomplish any particular goal. Positive affirmations may include visualizations, writing positive statements in a notebook, or even saying them aloud each day. The end goal of this type of positive thinking is to gain the self confidence you need to accomplish what you want. It also has the effect of countering some of the negative statements that you hear each day. Using these techniques effectively can gain you a competitive edge. In every area of life you will be much happier with a positive attitude and high level of self confidence. It's possible that a positive attitude can even improve your health in addition to raising your level of happiness by reducing the stress you carry around each day. Even if I'm just happier, isn't it worth it? Other people want to be around a happy positive person and that's just the honest truth. I will always try to limit the amount of time I spend with someone who is always negative.

Through positive thinking and positive affirmations, I have been able to boost my excitement and energy when facing challenges and turn failure into success. If you aren't one of the few who already use positive affirmations to develop a high level of self confidence, you can still benefit. This is because a positive way of thinking is something that is taught, not something that is inherited. Your thought process can change if you want it to be, you simply have to choose. It isn't like being born with brown eyes or red hair – it's something that is totally and completely under your control. I remind myself and practice this regularly.

Everything you need to reroute yourself onto a more healthy, functional and productive path is already inside you. I had learn to respond differently to opinions that don't matter and are likely based on past performance. Your past is no indicator of your future and to get different results you can start right now, today. People can change their behaviors, habits and tendencies and they do it all the time. The past is the past and nothing more.

One of the biggest insecurities I've found among people who doubt their abilities is that the lack of formal education. Let me tell you that it isn't necessary to have a master's degree to earn six figures annually. Believe me, I know. I don't have the high level formal education most people equate with a large income and a comfortable living, but I didn't let it stop me. No formal education is necessary to live the life of your dreams. In reality, it's just an excuse, but millions of people feel less than adequate either due to education or for some other reason. Unfortunately, that emotion keeps them working hard, earning little and wishing they had some way out.

Self-Esteem

It's easy to say that you should use criticisms to motivate, you shouldn't let negative comments hold you back and that everything you need to get the life you want is already in you, but believing it requires that you have a high level of self-esteem. Self-esteem is what you think about yourself as a person and if you think you are a loser, you are. Conversely, if you think you are valuable and can accomplish great things, you will. You don't always have control over what thoughts enter your head. But you do have control over how long you entertain them and how long you wait to change them if at all.

To know how to raise your self-esteem, you have to first know what goes into it. Your self-esteem includes your opinions about yourself, your personality, your body and what you look like. Your self-esteem also includes what you think others think of you as a person, how much you like yourself and how much you think others like you. If you are still dwelling on negative thoughts and ideas about yourself, then you have some rebuilding of your self-esteem to do. A healthy self-esteem is needed to produce accurate and constructive views of your abilities and to work toward your goals successfully. Otherwise, you will believe everything is outside your range of abilities and you will float through life letting it happen to you instead of taking control and determining your own destiny.

Let's take someone who has just given their first presentation at work and see how this person could use the experience to raise their self-esteem. Let's say this person did a poor job of presenting their ideas and was a noticeably bad public speaker. The first thing I would advise is focusing on the positive. If this person bombed, they should spend time complimenting themselves for having the courage to get up in front of a large group to present their ideas. This is a big fear for most people. They should think about how they're taking important steps in their career by beginning to give presentations. They should think about why they were asked or were chosen to give the presentation in the first place. Obviously they had some system, idea or finding that was important enough to share with others within the company. There are plenty of positives to see even within a bad experience.

If this person is being hard on themselves internally, they should stop the negative comments cold. People, especially those with low self-esteem, can easily be their toughest critic. They may zero in on the weakness and be overly hard on themselves. Realize what you're saying to yourself and how harmful those ideas are. Now imagine those things you're saying to yourself are actually coming from a coworker and are being directed at someone else. Wouldn't you likely step in and say that they are being way too critical? Why not give yourself that same amount of respect and stop your own harsh criticisms? If anyone else spoke to us the way we sometimes speak to ourselves, we would be offended. Stop it!

This presenter would also benefit greatly from cutting out all the exaggerations and needlessly "final" statements. They may be saying to themselves, "I knew that was going to go badly. I've never been a good public speaker and I never will be. They'll never ask me to do that again." There is much room for improvement in those statements. The presenter should not be so final with negative comments, such as when he says he'll *never* be a good public speaker and his bosses will *never* ask him to step forward and give a presentation again. He might as well be saying that he's *always* going to screw up that part of his job. If that's what he believes, that's probably what will happen. Of all the possible self-fulfilling prophecies to mutter to yourself, why choose such a negative one? Think=Action=Results.

This person should accept that they are learning and accept the fact that they are human and are going to mess up from time to time, but it is unhealthy to assume that you will always mess up. Everyone has bad days and everyone can choose to forgive themselves. If the presenter was very nervous, they should forgive that. It happens to anyone who isn't comfortable speaking in public. This person could join Toastmasters or other organizations that specialize in helping people learn the skills to be good public speakers. Practice on your own by challenging yourself to strike up conversations with strangers until you have overcome your fear of them.

I remember some time ago I had to give a speech. It was supposed to be about 30 minutes long. I was very nervous and when the time came I spoke very quickly and emotionally. I was done in about 12 minutes! I thought I had done badly and maybe I did, but there were many people in the audience that said it was great and encouraged me to do it again sometime. Today I speak frequently and have become relaxed and comfortable. Practice makes perfect. Many people fear public speaking and I've heard its higher on some people's 'fear list' than dying. Wow! So the guy giving the funeral eulogy would probably rather be in the coffin than give the speech!

Replacing criticism with encouragement would provide the presenter another boost to one's self-esteem. They might be replacing comments like, "I wasn't good on my feet" to something along the lines of, "I will do better next time if I take a breath and relax." It's unnecessary to beat yourself up over things that can be fixed with a few words of encouragement. What's done is done.

Part of correcting mistakes is taking responsibility for them in the first place. But in order to have a healthy level of self-esteem, you have to avoid taking responsibility for everything that goes wrong. The projector bulb burning out halfway through the presentation isn't the fault of the presenter. If you try to take responsibility for everything, you will burden yourself beyond what anybody would be able to handle. Try to view things without bias and assess the situation objectively when things go wrong rather than just assuming you made an error.

It takes practice to change your attitude and adopt a positive mindset. But as you start implementing it, you will find that it gets easier with time. You will also find that you new found positivity rubs off on others creating a supportive network of those who are positive. This helps you as well as helping them by decreasing your daily does of negativity.

The bottom line is that you can do anything as long as you believe it is possible. It's this belief that saw me through the tough times when I wanted to give up. The path to success isn't easy, but easy accomplishments aren't rewarding. It is only when you strive for more that you feel the personal fulfillment of success in many areas of your life.

Chapter 5
Making Sense of Things

Charles Whyte

Chapter 5
Making Sense of Things

If you, in your career, feel a great deal of uncertainty, you can change that by adjusting your attitude in a few important areas. The first is to look at your past experiences. I know that there were times, especially during my younger years, that I blamed others for where I was. I now know that much of the time it really was my fault. It's easy to shift this blame as it lessens the burden we feel when we can convince ourselves that it's someone else's fault. I remember that I had a boss once that I thought was a jerk and after I lost that job, I blamed him for a long time. As I reflected on the situation some time later, I realized that I was the jerk and he was just doing his job. When I let go of my anger at him, I immediately started to feel better. I knew that I was changing, especially my attitude, and this made for a happier me. But it isn't healthy to blame others and we can't begin to make healthier decisions until we accept responsibility for our lives.

You may not have an addiction that you blame on others, but there is likely something that you have hard feelings about. We've all at some point been hurt by the actions or words of another. Maybe you are forced to deal with a gossipy coworker or your mother is overly critical of your chosen career. It may be that a supervisor took credit for something you did or an idea you shared. Perhaps a personal relationship went awry and someone you once loved did or said some very hurtful things. It could be anything and almost everyone will have their own unique story of betrayal or hurt feelings. But if you never practice the act of forgiveness, you only make yourself a victim to act over and over with no end. You aren't hurting them by holding onto your hurt feelings; you are only hurting yourself.

Forgiveness, just so we're clear, is the act of releasing your grip on those resentments and thoughts of revenge. It's not about pretending you agree with that person's actions or saying that what they did was okay. It's just releasing your own hurt. When you harbour those feelings and frequently reflect on them, you are bound to that time and to the event that hurt you so deeply. You are unable to break free and move on and moving on for me was a must!

Assessing the cause of your feelings of resentment and anger is part of getting over it. But if you never step beyond that, the first step of recovery, then you will never grow from that experience. When you find what or who you feel to be the source of your pain and anguish, you've taken one important step toward mending the situation, but you cannot call it good at assessing blame. Blame does not mend any situation. It never has and it never will. Assessing blame is a lot like an alcoholic coming to the realization that they are an alcoholic and never taking any further steps toward recovery. Blaming and then revisiting that blame constantly without ever taking another step will only breed bad moods and negative thoughts.

This crankiness will hurt your personal relationships and even have negative physiological affects like higher blood pressure, faster heart rate, chronic pain and symptoms of anxiety and depression. These physical signs may be mild at first, but realize that resentments have a cumulative effect on your mind and body. You can see how refusing to move past the blame stage to the forgiveness stage hurts you and it can cause a tremendous amount of damage.

Through forgiveness, we are able to block those negative, resentful feelings from showing up in relationships. We're healthier and more likeable when we're able to stop dwelling on how we have been hurt by others and how angry that makes us feel.

Forgive Yourself

When I have decided that someone else is to blame and proved repeatedly to you I'm not capable of getting over it, I'm admitting that I don't have the ability or control to determine my own situation in life.

By never moving beyond my hurt feelings and resentments, I'm giving that other person or situation control over my life. A parent who mistreated you growing up and may have contributed to a harmful addiction by putting a beer in your hand at age 11 may create some understandable resentment or even anger. But that doesn't mean I don't have a choice right now today.

What happened in the past is in the past and I can choose how I will proceed. You can choose to move past anything that has or will happen to you. When you throw your hands up and say your parents put you where you are, you are not exercising that power over your life. It's your life. I had many issues growing up, but if I had not decided to forgive and move on, I would still be back where I was – an angry resentful young man wasting my energy on negativity and getting nowhere.

In order to take control, you have to accept the fact that your current situation may not be what you want it to be, that it may not be entirely your fault and let it go. Certain things in life are out of your control, but what you do with your life isn't one of those things that your parents or anybody else determines. Accept that things may be difficult for you, but that they are also within your power to change if you so choose. Any problem, business, relationships, finances – all of these can be changed if you choose. Change is inevitable; I want it to be positive.

Some of the hardest events or issues to move past are those that you bring on yourself. It's one thing to let go of emotions or to forgive another person, but completely different if the person to forgive is yourself. For example, if a high school-aged person becomes pregnant or gets someone else pregnant, they may find themselves working menial jobs because the child's needs took all the finances, time and energy they could have used to get a good formal education and begin a career. This is a big burden and feeds into our sense of 'deservedness'. You may think, "I don't deserve to move on since I created this problem myself." The situation is much the same as blaming someone else for your travails. You are telling yourself that you're where you are in life because of your actions or someone else's and believe that you don't have the power to set things right.

This happens in both big and small ways in almost everyone's life. No matter the situation, you must accept that yes, the event happened and perhaps you could have made better decisions, but that doesn't mean you can't learn from it and move on. By forgiving yourself, you put those hard feelings in your past and set yourself free. Life moves on no matter how good or bad we deal with it, and you have an opportunity today to change your choices and actions to get better results.

Being angry and bitter do nothing but handicap your ability to think clearly and to reason appropriately when faced with many of life's decisions. You stepped up and are doing what needs to be done. Now move on. I mean really move on; let it go; fight the urge to recycle it and start now to make real progress.

Acting out of revenge, like leaving a lucrative job over a dispute with a coworker or supervisor, can have disastrous effects on your life. If you were unfairly fired from your job and now are in danger of losing your house, giving up and being foreclosed on because you're sad and angry about it will make your life harder in the coming months than it would be if you had dealt with the situation logically and looked for solutions. It is common when something happens to be so wrapped up in emotion that it almost paralyzes you. The best defense is to recognize this for what it is and release those emotions. Ask someone else (not involved in the situation) for their opinion, get their advice. Stop, take a breath, calm down and make a plan of action.

Additionally, it may help you to know that assigning blame to yourself, and then obsessing about it, is also a type of self-pity. You feel sorry for yourself and become convinced that not only can you not move forward, you can't correct anything or make things any better – but this is a lie. It allows us to pass the responsibility on to others and also excuses us of the work it takes to correct our circumstances. Let it go! Remember, tomorrow is a new day. And it will arrive whether you are prepared or not, so why not start fresh and with a plan?

By freeing yourself of that tendency to blame, you are able to move on to the next stage of personal growth, and letting those negative emotions go becomes even easier.

Charles Whyte

The Up Side of Failure

You may be dealing with unemployment and the host of problems that can develop from it. You may be facing a foreclosure and have no place for you and your family to live. You may find yourself working at a job with no opportunity for advancement, feeling stuck and living paycheck to paycheck. Maybe you have a debilitating disease such as multiple sclerosis or have endured a significant injury that has hampered your mobility. Maybe you're like I was and are trying to beat an addiction. It could be any circumstance that keeps you from accomplishing your life goals.

Remember that no matter what you're up against, someone else has experienced the same situation and beaten it. Google the term 'inspirational story' sometime. Suddenly you won't think that losing your job is something from which you can't recover or that dealing with arthritis in your hands will result in an incredibly difficult life. Stories abound of people taking responsibility for their emotions and improving their lives no matter the circumstance. You can really put things in perspective by learning what others have experienced.

A good example is Carrie Johnson, an Olympian kayaker who competes despite being diagnosed with the debilitating and even life-threatening Crohn's disease. And almost everyone knows Lance Armstrong's story. He was diagnosed with testicular cancer that had spread to his abdomen, lungs and brain. After going through the difficult treatment, Armstrong came back and won multiple Tours de France. Jackie Robinson, the first black player in Major League Baseball, faced constant threats against his life and felt lonely and isolated as both fellow players and even coaches didn't want him on their team. If you familiarize yourself with these stories or any of the hundreds like them, there's no reason to believe that you can't overcome any issues or challenges in your life.

This was true for me as well. I've always been active but over the years all the activities and abuse from smaller injuries have taken their toll on my hips. A few years ago, it got to the point I struggled to walk without pain. Sometimes I could get by fine, but more and more of the time my hips interfered with my normal life. I had to make the decision to have the issue corrected and for me that meant at least six weeks at home while one hip was replaced and then six more weeks while the other was replaced.

It wasn't easy. I was on crutches, but I hobbled around and recuperated quite well. But had I not made the choices that allowed me to work from home during that time it may not have happened when I needed it to happen. It was a big challenge and literally months out of my life for recovery but I faced it with a positive outcome and had a tremendous result. Today, I live pain free and have total mobility. It's as if I never had a problem with my hips. This is all due to the fact that I chose to face this problem head on and do something about it.

A large part of overcoming obstacles, regardless of what they are, is viewing them with a positive attitude. It's difficult to do when you've had your home foreclosed on, lost your job or routinely made poor life decisions in the past, but a positive attitude will show your desire to work toward a solution. With the right attitude, a failure is just a learning experience. It will reveal to you things that you have done wrong that you can apply to your later life experiences.

After beating an addiction to drugs and alcohol, I learned the importance of having healthy habits. I learned that I should surround myself with friends that provide a positive influence. I learned that anything worth accomplishing requires hard work. These are lessons that I can apply to just about every challenge I face in my professional and personal life – not just when it comes to avoiding a relapse. They embody the very essence of the belief that failure is just the opportunity to begin again with more intelligence.

Sometimes those things that seem to be big mistakes actually turn out to be wonderful business opportunities. Not long ago I met a man named Dan who owned a granite countertop company. He revealed to me the interesting way in which his business came about. Several years ago, he worked for a similar company that worked with a range of materials from granite to marble to tile. While on a job that he felt was done unsatisfactorily, he openly criticized the company he worked for and the quality of work they had done on this job. Little did he know, his cell phone was on a call directly to the boss and owner of the company that employed him and the boss hear him speak candidly and very unflatteringly about his employer and the quality of work he had seen done with this client. Dan was fired immediately. Remember to make sure your cell phone is off if you are going to badmouth your employer! Or better yet, hold your tongue completely.

Having lost his job, Dan was forced to find a new source of income. This could be devastating for anyone in this situation, but instead of becoming paralyzed, Dan started his own granite countertop company that would focus on one material and thus do a better job with installations. Today, Dan is his own boss and easily earns six figures a year. Rather than hang onto negative emotions from his firing, Dan instead saw the opportunity to start his own company using the knowledge he had gained from his previous employer.

His story is much the same as JetBlue honcho David Neeleman. Neeleman's story includes multiple failures, including his first startup in his twenties that failed miserably. He was running an airline company that flew exclusively from the west coast to Hawaii when a supplier they used went out of business. His company, in turn, was forced out of business, having lost a large amount of money by signing a contract with a vendor who went out of business shortly thereafter. Neeleman found his way to a small airline, Morris Air, which had to take on investors to get started. After a few successful years, Morris Air sold to Southwest Airlines for $130 million. As the second largest investor in the company, Neeleman was a millionaire many times over. Neeleman could have allowed his confidence to be shattered when his own company went under, but he started over and made millions doing so.

After Morris Air, Neeleman went to work for Southwest Airlines. He signed a five year contract, which included a non-compete clause. After only a few months, Neeleman was let go. Forced out of the airline industry for another four and a half years due to his no-compete clause, Neeleman could have easily soured on the airline industry altogether and walked away a millionaire. But instead he took four and a half years to put together yet another airline. When his no-compete clause expired, JetBlue was able to take to the skies. Neeleman's philosophy about failure is that it happens to everyone at some point, but how you react to it is what makes you. You can see a failure as devastating, pity yourself and place blame on others or you can see it as an opportunity to start fresh, to undertake a new venture, to use what you've learned to reach even higher.

It's a stance that I have a hard time arguing against as I feel a failure isn't a failure until you accept it as such and quit trying. Failure is temporary; giving up makes it permanent. When you say that you cannot do any better or that you cannot do it again, you can't apply what you've learned, you can't be successful, you just can't do it – that's when you truly fail in life. Until you've reached that point, you are merely taking life's journey. It's important to remember that a failure is only devastating if you allow it to be. Until then, it's just a setback.

No one who ever does anything significant with their lives, be it start a big company or earn a great deal of money or beat a devastating disease or addiction, is perfect. Everyone is going to make mistakes, misjudgments, bad decisions and even find themselves facing adversity through no fault of their own. Failure, mistakes and adversity are all part of life and no matter how hard we try to avoid them, we're going to have to overcome those challenges at some point.

Obstacle = Opportunity

The right attitude to take when you face failure, or as I like to call it, an obstacle, is to think of it as nothing more than an opportunity. The next rock in your path might turn out to be a stepping stone. If you're able to see the positive when you reach one of life's many obstacles, then congratulate yourself on taking the healthy approach. This way of thinking will benefit you in the end, rather than handicap any chance you have because you're sorrowful and angry to have reached one of life's challenging situations. How dare anything bad happen to you now!

Obstacles are part of life and nothing more than a chance for you to create an exciting new chapter in your eventual autobiography. We all want one of those, don't we? I will admit, though, that I used to encounter a challenge, sigh loudly and ask to no one in particular, "Why me?" or "Why now?" What I didn't realize at the time is that these obstacles were inescapable and I hurt only myself by seeing them as anything less than something that I had no choice but to push through. I realized in time that one's mindset is all that stands between seeing your failures as obstacles and your obstacles as opportunities.

Most of us at some point have had car trouble. It seems that it always comes at the worst possible time, too. Your car smokes and won't run in the middle of a long trip to your favorite vacation spot. Your battery dies at work or your check engine light comes on the minute you turn on the engine. There are many ways to react to this situation and most often it's with anger or frustration. I know this has been my initial reaction many a time.

For me, I have found an effective response is to just deal with the obstacle. Call an auto club and get a tow. Have a mechanic check the vehicle. It's possible that the problem could be minor or it could signal a possible larger problem that you are able to identify early that could have cost hundreds if not thousands of dollars to repair later if you had not discovered it. The end result is that you were set back a few hours and you encountered some unforeseen expenses, but you are able to continue from that point knowing that the car is in better shape now that it has been repaired and given a once-over by a trained mechanic. From that point, you may find that you feel secure knowing your car will likely be fine for some time to come.

Comparable occurrences happen all the time in our professional lives. You may find yourself doing your supervisor's job for a fraction of the pay. If that supervisor comes along and criticizes the quality of your work, it could be damaging to your self-esteem. It could cause hurt feelings and anger, quite easily, toward your boss. It would benefit you to think of the criticisms as direction or 'course correction' for the next time you "do their work." And instead of thinking to yourself that you're doing their work and that if they don't like it, that they should do it themselves, you could instead think that they presented you with an opportunity. It's unlikely that your supervisor is attempting to pass your work off as their own. They may be extending a challenge to you. They may be seeing if you're capable of management. It's an opportunity to display your competence and ability to take another step forward in your career.

Your first reaction would probably be to think that your boss dislikes you, is treating you like a temp or is punishing you for some unknown wrongdoing. It's an unhealthy point of view to take, particularly that latter – that you are being punished. You begin to think about what you could have possibly done wrong to deserve such treatment and may begin to second guess yourself and read too much into little things. It may also cause enough animosity for your boss to realize that you get angry when they ask you to do anything extra – this can bring on disastrous consequences as now your negative emotions may cost you a promotion or even your job.

Viewing the events as an opportunity to grow into a greater role in your company will allow you to complete your assignments with a much healthier and therefore much more productive mindset. It will also provide you with experience you need if you ever wish to advance in your chosen field. When I had to go on full commission it was a frightening and uncertain time. It was hard to let go of steady money, but the opportunity held tremendous promise and was committed to making it work. Had I only delivered a half effort, I would have surely failed. What to do? I shook off the fear, which was like a huge weight. It was not easy; I felt so scared sometimes that it was like walking in quicksand, but quitting was not an option. So I put on blinders, dug in and focused on what I had to do. Every once in a while the fear would creep back in, but I would force it right back out of my mind. I started slowly building up a reserve of my commissions, not taking it all at once. The reserve was small at first, but eventually grew to a size that let me know I would be alright for the short term and them even longer. This also helped me sleep at night and made it possible not to worry and do the work needed. Eventually, I became more confident and less fearful, but it took time and effort.

Going forward, if you choose to stay in your field, even if it isn't with that same company, you will feel more competent and capable in your abilities to succeed. Taking a healthier approach benefits you tremendously in this respect. You have more confidence in yourself to do the job, even if it's the job of management and that you'll be fine even if you should move on from your current employer for any reason. And for the time that you remain with your current employer, you will likely feel more confident because you feel the supervisor turns to you for help when they need it. You will feel more secure knowing that you are an important part of your company's structure. You will feel as though you are the one given responsibilities over your coworkers. In this case, you should view your newly acquired expectations as a reason to feel a greater sense of pride in yourself. I did, and the rewards have been worth it!

Chapter 6
The Company You Keep

Charles Whyte

Chapter 6

The Company You Keep

Tell me what company you keep and I'll tell you who you are. It's a generalization that we've all heard, but you have to admit that there's some truth to it. It may not be absolutely necessary in every case to change who you associate with to accomplish your specific goals, but it definitely makes things easier if they take away from your drive. If your goal in life right now is a difficult one, then why make it that much harder to accomplish by associating with those who are going to act as opposition?

For example, a young girl grows up in a very conservative part of the country where the accepted norm is that men earn a living and women keep the home. This young girl may witness her mother staying at home and being the homemaker despite a desire to have her own career. As the girl grows into adulthood, she may become friends with classmates who possess those conservative viewpoints themselves – that women are homemakers and men are breadwinners. This girl may give into external pressures to marry, submit to the wishes of her husband and keep the home. This girl, now a grown woman, may tire of this system and wish to break from tradition and earn a living. The response from her family, her husband, her children and her friends may not be positive. They will probably think that what she wants is wrong or strange. They may not understand her need to accomplish more with her life and refuse to support her attempts to pursue a career. This young woman will probably meet resistance from virtually everyone she knows if she attempts to start a career.

It's not just addicts that have to worry about acquaintances dragging them back into old habits and dashing any possibility of a positive outcome. Many of us are immersed in very negative environments and this has an effect on you. Everyone with virtually any kind of goal can meet resistance from those around them. Whether you want to chase the dream of owning your own design firm or you want to go to law school; whether you want to have a healthy relationship with your spouse or you want to live in the elite neighborhood in your town, you need people around you that have similar goals, or at least support your pursuit, in order to improve your chances of accomplishing it. If you continue to associate with those who don't understand or don't support your bid to accomplish your dream, you are inviting opposition and negativity. You are needlessly making things more difficult for yourself.

Benefits of a Good Support System

A true support system means you have individuals in your life that believe in your ability to accomplish your goals and will encourage you to keep going even when things get difficult. And when you're trying to change your life, things will get difficult. If you lack that support system, those around you will try to drag you back into your old, destructive or disagreeable habits – or worse, they will convince you to give up completely and just accept the status quo.

For example, the young woman who wants to start a career instead of keep a home would be welcomed back into community of conservative family models the first time she displays a wavering attitude or a change of heart, however temporary. Those of us who are trying to change our situations for the better are going to have times like these when we want to back out or revert to the old, comfortable way of doing things. When those around us discourage us or allow us to quit on ourselves, they are proving themselves to be disbelievers and detractors.

It is important that you strive to surround yourself with people who will give you encouragement when you face challenges in your life. They can hear out this momentary breakdown in your will before helping you regain your desire to change. Just like a boxer may need a second wind to defeat a challenging opponent, you may need a mid-fight pep talk from a trusted friend to get back the drive to deal with the challenges you face. Whether this support system takes the tough love approach or a soft and encouraging tone, you need someone to believe in you and convince you that your goals are still worth struggling to accomplish. While you sometimes can't completely get away from your detractors (family is family after all), you can dilute their negative comments by adding people into your life that are encouraging and have been down the same path.

I remember when I first started in sales. My boss, a very good salesperson himself, told me, "Just be yourself and don't lie – it will always catch up with you. If you are yourself and not some thought up idea of what you think a salesperson is, then people will like you and deal with the real you. Not everyone will like you, but the ones who do will be liking the real you. It's so much easier just to be yourself." In time, because I was very aware of my actions, I think I became a better person.

Of course there is no question that I've created some of the challenges in my life – especially early on. Even when you make mistakes, I find it invaluable to be able to talk to someone who doesn't judge you and who understands what it's like to try and change. Years ago, even when I didn't believe in myself and was submitting to the process of change for all the wrong reasons, I was encouraged by someone who had been in my shoes and knew I could succeed. These days, I'm very aware of not judging people by their mistakes. We all have the ability to change, but it can be very difficult when you don't have that encouragement and the strength of others to rely on when it would be easy to go back to what you have known before.

The best people for the job of supporting you through change are usually the ones who have experience in whatever it is you are trying to accomplish and can not only encourage, but offer sound experienced advice. One of the easiest ways to succeed is to surround yourself with those that have been successful at what it is you want to do. Someone whose circumstances were at one time the same as yours are now, but who overcame them, will be such a source of inspiration to you. Some call these people mentors and they can drastically increase your chances of success. Odds are that those people who are wildly successful have had a mentor at some point in their lives and often they are eager to mentor others as well.

There are typically two ways to learn in life. You can either learn from your own mistakes or learn from the mistakes of others. A mentor will provide you with the knowledge and advice that will allow you to learn from their mistakes, which is what everyone should strive to do. Imagine the pain and loss you would avoid by learning from a mentor's experiences rather than your own. Their leadership in this regard is invaluable. They can supply the knowledge, support and resources you are going to need to meet each challenge that awaits you.

Mentors are also able to provide you that sometimes brutal honesty you may not get elsewhere. While doling out criticisms can bruise egos, suggestions from a mentor are meant to motivate you and make you aware of changes that need to be made. It's true that a criticism can be crippling and create hard feelings between mentor and pupil, but mentors understand that a day or two of hurt feelings is better than allowing you to fail and go on with an unfulfilled life. A good mentor will not spare your feelings so that you will be aware of your strengths and weaknesses and will be there to remind you that failure is temporary while quitting makes it permanent.

Equipped with this knowledge of your strengths and weaknesses, you are able to develop your strengths and minimize if not eliminate your weaknesses. By bringing out what you're good at and making you almost hyper-vigilant of your weaknesses, you know where to seek the help you need and where to take over to increase your chances of success. In the end, a mentor knows that they are not your friend first and that you will not "like" them all the time and this is okay because they are solely focused on your success. I know that my experience with a family mentor has been good. They know me as well as anyone, yet can still be honest about any weakness they observe.

If you don't have a mentor, the next best thing is a truly good friend or family member. These people can be trusted to provide support and encouragement to keep you going in the face of so many obstacles. These are more readily available, since everyone has a friend or family member that they can turn to. You can rely on them as long as they are true to you and can eventually come to terms with the fact that you are attempting to change yourself. Sometimes they'll view it as losing a friend or loved one as you "leave behind the person they know."

A friend or family member can act as that other head and you know what they say about two heads: they are better than one. But you still must be aware of their limitations. If they don't have experience in the area you are pursuing, their advice will be based on their background – which may not be successful. A friend or family member may not be able to guide you to a good but thrifty lawyer to establish your company or write you that requisite recommendation letter to get a loan, but they are great sounding boards for your ideas, hopes and opinions. When you need emotional guidance and assistance, they can give you that, but you might be surprised at their experience in matters you never knew they had to deal with like employees or customers.

Making Good Connections

If everyone had a good support system already in place, much more would be accomplished in the world. But too often we find that we don't have the right kind of people surrounding us to do with our lives what we'd really like to. That's why it's so important to take a look at the relationships in your life and ask yourself if they are going to help or hurt your attempts to take significant steps in fulfilling your dreams. We would all benefit by taking some time to examine the merits of the relationships we have in our lives before setting our plans into motion. Will they poison our chances for success or will they make us stronger?

While a mentor isn't a friend and therefore does not see you for your past, a friend or family member might. It's possible that they may see you as that same childhood friend they used to play ball with on the playground or the helpless infant they cared for. This can take away from their ability to be the right kind of support, so it's the one caveat of the friend and family member support system.

When your resilience is tested in your attempts to change, a family member's initial reaction may be to coddle, comfort and go along with whatever makes you happy or gives you relief. If you are at a point where you are questioning your ability to succeed, a family member or friend may be too willing to let you off the hook. If you feel or have experienced this behavior, know that the right kind of person may not adjust well at first to your attempts to change. It may be hard sometimes for them to watch you change, and possibly move on, to become someone more than they are used to.

Some people will allow you to quit on yourself because they are not capable of being supportive or can't be the right kind of support for you. If they are unable to separate you from the person you're trying to be, then it can be a sign they are unwilling to consider you anything but that person and they are not going to be a positive influence. If you find yourself in this kind of relationship with anyone, you need to know that time with this person should be very limited if not entirely eliminated. They will have a damaging effect on your attempts, will subtly, though maybe not purposely, attempt to dissuade you from changing in order to keep you in the mold they've always known and been comfortable with.

I've seen this happen with siblings. There are two brothers I know, we'll them Jim and Ron. The brothers always got along well and were close. Jim is the older brother and has always been the dominant personality. He was captain of the football team and very popular when they were in school. Jim got a sports scholarship to college, but never finished his degree and has been a car salesman at a local dealership for more than fifteen years.

Ron was always more contemplative. He studied hard and got good grades. He received an academic scholarship and graduated with a business degree. Right out of school, Ron went to work for a large accounting firm.

For ten years, the situation remained the same between the brothers where Jim made more money and was well-known in the community. But several years ago, Ron decided to leave his accounting firm and start his own real estate investment business. You would think that Jim would be his biggest supporter, but it was just the opposite. Jim was very critical of Ron and constantly berated his attempts in real estate as irresponsible. Jim said that Ron had a good solid job and he'd just thrown it away on a pipe dream. This tension caused a rift between the brothers.

Ron went on to become very successful at real estate and is now a millionaire, while Jim is still working at the dealership. Here again, you'd think Jim would be happy for his brother, but it has completely changed their relationship as Jim can't handle the idea that his little brother is doing better than him. It's taken about four years for them to improve their relationship, but it took a great deal of effort.

The right friend, the right family member, the person who will provide the kind of support you need will always come around in the end, but that doesn't mean it will be a smooth ride. If you have a friend or family member who refuses to see you in any light other than one in which they've always known you, it doesn't necessarily mean that they're not on your side. They could come around at any point. Don't be too quick to cut certain friends and family from your life if they do not immediately adjust to the new life plan you've created. You can just temporarily distance yourself and then later, when they come around you can renew the relationship.

To identify a good friend who will be an asset to you going forward, ask yourself if you have a close enough relationship with this person to exchange constructive criticism. Just like a mentor will put your friendship aside to tell you how it is, it's always a good thing to have a friend who can do this as well. And that goes for your life in general, not just when you've set forth a plan to change yourself. A friend who can be honest with you can tell you when you are making a wrong move or are acting based on faulty reasoning is someone worth keeping in your life.

Everyone has those friends who are somewhere between true friend and acquaintance. You spend a fair amount of time with them, but there is something standing between your ability to be truly honest with one another. Maybe there has not been that bonding experience yet in your relationship. If they cannot provide you the kind of honest feedback and advice that you seek, they fall in the "unable" or "unwilling" category when it comes to finding your support system. Ask yourself if you can see them being a willing and helpful part of your life as you make drastic changes.

It's also good to consider your relationships with others and try to put yourselves in their shoes. Ask yourself how they really see you. Gaining an understanding of how others see you will help you understand their point of view and why they react to you and your opinions the way they do. If you believe that they see you as someone who lacks a good work ethic, then you can address those concerns and you can work hard to correct that belief. If you believe that people doubt your ability to get into and succeed in attaining higher education, do well on your entrance exams and prove them wrong. By knowing why the close relationships around may not be the strongest or even have a solid foundation to be of help for you when you need them, you can work to create trust and turn nonbelievers into your biggest cheerleaders.

It's in your best interest to correct and strengthen these relationships now. You don't want to find out later that the advice and feedback you get from those around you is skewed by an inability to see you in a different light or because they are skeptical of your abilities. Mom seeing you as her little baby will have an impact on the advice and guidance she provides. Your friend seeing you as that crazy guy they used to drink with in college will have an impact on the feedback and support he gives you as well. Look at these relationships, how they function, and determine if they will derail you later and if you can change them.

When You Can't

If you've looked at all of your relationships, chances are you have identified one or two that will be a detriment to your progress. It's just going to happen. Because people's opinions about you, whether or not they have merit, drastically change your interactions with them.

But what are you to do when that relationship can't be changed and it can't be eliminated either? What if your college-aged daughter will always see you as mom and that, despite the fact that you want to challenge yourself with a new career, thinks you should be available at a moment's notice to help her through the difficult transition of home life to college life? What if your business partner doesn't understand your desire to begin leading a healthier lifestyle and will not adapt their daily routine to exclude cigarettes and fast food?

Obviously your relationship with your child is unbreakable. If you are in the office nine hours a day with your business partner, you really can't sell your interest in the company just to escape the daily temptation of a Whopper and a few Marlboros. Sometimes it's you that needs to change, adapt and stay motivated in the face of temptations and the demands of others.

When you know that you will face these challenges and a few uphill battles, it's always a good idea to clearly define your goals. You aren't likely to accomplish your goals if they are simply vague ideas that you've never worked through and they can easily crumble in the face of criticism.

When you force your goals to the forefront of your consciousness, they're there when you encounter life decisions that might impact those goals. You are more likely to make the right decision, one that agrees with your goal, when you are actively thinking about it and consciously aware of what you really want. For example, if you want an advanced degree, you will define in what field, from what college, and what exams need to be taken to get into that graduate school. If something like a usual family vacation conflicted with classes, you would choose to reschedule the vacation rather than the degree.

I know for myself when I started in sales I had to spend many nights with my boss learning the ins and outs of why a job costs this much or that much and where the numbers came from. He also suggested that I take a salesmanship course of some sort. So, I enrolled in an evening course at a local college. I had small children at home and knew this would conflict with my normal family time, but I also knew this sacrifice needed to be made in order to progress and become a better, more valuable salesperson. This, and the long hours with my boss, would pay dividends in the long run and my family would enjoy those benefits as well.

This type of focused decision making helps in your personal relationships in much the same way. Spending a great deal of time with a friend who doesn't put much stock in academia would be a bad influence on the person who dreams of an advanced degree. If you continue to spend time with this friend, you can see their desire to spend time shopping and watching numerous movies as detrimental to what you want to accomplish. Instead, you may choose to limit your time with them to weekend outings which can be a departure from the hard work of studying and striving to accomplish your goals – a kind of treat at the end of the week. Viewing the relationship in a new light and being aware of when and how it can throw your chances of success off will help you avoid falling into the traps it presents in your life.

You can see how your goals will play into your plans and thought processes on many levels when you are actively thinking about them and you can't actively think about them until they are clearly defined. Being cognizant of your exact goal is a larger piece of the battle for success than most people think. When I went through that low time in my life, I wanted to make things better for me and my children. This idea was a constant great motivator for me and because of it, I went out and got that old blue car and kept it looking decent with my duct tape and spray paint repairs.

As part of making my life better, I also wanted to spend time with my children, but had no money, which meant I had to be creative. It would have been easy to allow my embarrassment at my financial situation be an excuse for me not to make such efforts, but a good relationship with my children was part of my long term plan and they were a huge part of what kept me going. I simply identified the challenge, decided on a plan of action and found a way to get it done.

You can make these goals a part of your thought pattern in many ways. Some keep visualization books where they write down their specific goal and even include images of what they want. Some can simply make a list and keep it on the refrigerator or where they will see it often. Others will enter it into their journal and track their progress. It may help you to tell people about your goals so they can hold you accountable. Sometimes having it out there that you want to do something forces you to address it or deal with the follow up questions friends and family will shower you with for the next few years. You want to write a book? So you tell your family about it. Get ready to discuss your book and how it's coming along at every Christmas dinner for the next five years if you don't get busy and get it done. Everyone is different and the goal will become real to each of us in different ways. If necessary, experiment with various ways to make your goals something you will work toward.

Another great way to limit the effect of a damaging personal relationships is to remain strong in spite of them. Routinely reminding yourself of the times when a relationship can set you back will keep you aware and help you avoid the thought process that lets those relationships damage you. For example, a woman who wants to go to law school but has to deal with a mother who thinks that a woman's place is in the home would have to endure biting comments on many occasions. The next time her mother comments about ordering out for dinner instead of cooking for her family, she can take a deep breath and remind herself to be strong. The next time her mother has a cleaning tip and snidely asks her to pass it on to "the maid," because she hired a once-a-week cleaning service while she studies for her entrance exams, she'll know that a positive affirmation is in order and she can remind herself that those actions are helping her get to her goal. She can focus on the day when she has a successful law practice and how proud her mother will be then.

Hurtful comments and invitations to take steps backward are going to come up and may just be that person's inability to see you in a new light. It could take some adjusting and all you can do in the meantime is remind yourself that they are a distraction from your ultimate goal and everything they do and say to pull you down is a manifestation of that. Remain strong in your resolve; success may be around the very next corner.

Finally, know that your goals are within your reach. Everything you need to accomplish your goals and change your life is already in you. You have a clearly defined target to reach, the support system there to help you along the way and the motivation to get started and see it through to the end. Just buckle down and continue to strive. One little step or mini-plan at a time is all it takes to keep you moving forward toward your goals and before you know it you've climbed what looked like an insurmountable mountain.

I've spent quite a bit of time in the great outdoors, which includes climbing a few mountains. The funny thing is that when you are at the bottom looking up, the sun is in your eyes and you shade them to squint at that far away summit, the challenge seems huge. You wonder if you can do it and, even if you accomplish the climb, whether it will be worth it and whether you'll be in any shape to enjoy it. But once you persevere step by step up the steep slopes and you finally get to that summit and look down at that spot where you once stood, it doesn't seem that far. You feel the exhilaration and joy of accomplishment and the first thought that enters your mind is, "That wasn't nearly as hard as it looked!" This is often how we view life. Challenges and setbacks can seem like immovable objects that you will never overcome. Yet they are conquered just as any tall mountain – one small step at a time and the view from the top is breathtaking.

Chapter 7
You Come First

Charles Whyte

Chapter 7

You Come First

For so many years in my life I came first, meaning that I put my drinking and excesses before any other obligation or responsibility – the point that my wife at the time had enough. Many times I would leave people waiting for me to show up or do something, but I was not reliable because I was being selfish for all the wrong reasons and was not strong enough at the time to stop. After a while, no one really counted on me and that was a bad feeling. When I realized how my actions were being perceived by others, I decided that needed to change. I wanted to try to be that person they could count on and be proud of, but I had to work on myself to make that happen.

Think back to the last time you had the pleasure of traveling by plane. Do you remember the flight attendant's memorized pre-flight instructions? If you're a frequent traveler, you've probably learned to tune out the boring routine at the start of each flight, but you still know the drill. "This is how you buckle a seatbelt. Stow your luggage if you haven't already done so. Bring your seat back and folding trays to the full upright and locked position." But there's one instruction that I've always paid particularly close attention to: "In the event of cabin decompression, an oxygen mask will automatically drop from the compartment above your seat. To start the flow of oxygen, pull the mask toward you. Place it firmly over your nose and mouth, secure the elastic band behind your head, and breathe normally. Although the bag does not inflate, oxygen is flowing to the mask. If you are travelling with a child or someone who requires assistance, secure your mask first, and then assist the other person."

What it is about this part of the routine is the importance of securing your own mask before your own child's, if you should be traveling with them. It's not what most parents would consider their instant reaction to a potential disaster, but its reasoning is solid; you can't help anyone if you are not in a position to help. This often means taking care of yourself first. Even the Bible, indirectly, preaches taking care of yourself first. "Love thy neighbor as thyself." Though this is meant to say that you should care for others; it assumes that you first care for yourself. This is what I did. I started to take care of me so that I could be strong, healthy and educated for the journey ahead and, in doing so, make myself more valuable to the marketplace and to those I could help.

Psychologists call this principle "healthy selfishness" and would be quick to tell you that it can improve your quality of life by reducing stress, allowing you to enjoy your successes guilt-free and helping you to reach your full potential. It's something that I believe in wholeheartedly. Your goal may be that you would like to make a more comfortable living or that you would like to achieve more. In general, you would like to reach your full potential by accomplishing major life goals – be it by starting your own business or attaining a high-paying position within a company or industry. These goals require more than a little focus and care for yourself and I fully believe that you should indulge in healthy selfishness when it comes to the accomplishment of your goals.

This healthy selfishness, just so we're clear, is a mindset that allows you to pamper yourself,to separate yourself and rest if needed. To take the time to go to the gym or stop to read a book you have been looking forward to. Let's face it; we all need these times to recharge our batteries. We have to understand that we deserve this time for ourselves and we have earned it. It allows you to feel appreciation for your accomplishments. It allows you to care for yourself, your feelings, desires and needs. It gives you permission to respect your own opinions and trust your knowledge. It seems strange that you might need permission to act on your own behalf, nurture yourself, or love yourself unconditionally, but many people have a heavy load of guilt if they don't put everything and everyone before themselves. While this sounds noble, it is actually very dysfunctional as it doesn't nourish the source, which is you. In your everyday life, this can take on many forms. It may mean resting when you're tired. It may mean reducing your stress level, whatever that means to you. It may mean avoiding relationships with certain people who seem to invite chaos, or allow others the chance to solve their own problems without your assistance.

We do this to better our own situations because it's necessary to care for yourself, it's needed to reach your potential in life and it will probably allow you the ability to truly help those around that need your assistance. It will give you a life of freedom. It will give you freedom from the opinions and demands that others place on you. It will give you freedom from those overly-critical voices in your own head that judge and blame you.

You have to first get over the feeling that focusing on yourself is wrong and selfish. Improving yourself will make you better able to help those around you that you would like to help. With the right amount of foresight, you'll come to this same realization, just like the airline industry has come to the same realization regarding oxygen masks. You can't be much help to anybody if you're not in a position to help them adequately. It's a lot like scraping by financially and then loaning a friend a $200 to make his rent. Chances are that if you're barely capable of paying your own bills, loaning money to a friend is going to end disastrously for you.

By making your own situation secure and strong, you can help those around with money, support, time or whatever they need. This is something that I am always aware of because, at one time in my life, no one could have depended on me for hardly anything. There were also times when I had to depend on others just to get by. Now my family and friends know that I will always be there for them and this gives me comfort. There is no worse feeling than to see those you love suffer and know there is nothing you can do to help. It feels good for me just in the knowing I can support and care for others in my life, but it never would have happened had I not understood that I had to be strong and stable first.

Giving of yourself is like withdrawing money from a bank account. When you give to others, that energy flows out to them, depleting the source. But the sense of being there, being a rock for those in your life, fills you with renewed energy. If you constantly give without taking time to renew yourself, you get depleted both emotionally and physically. You have to take time to refill your spirit. This will often mean making your own personal "deposits" in the form of caring for ones' self, doing what you want to do and putting yourself before others at regular intervals. Giving of yourself need not be only financial. When I talk to someone and help them with their problems, my problems seem to be diminished and I often solve some of my own in this never ending learning process. Other people, even those in dire situations, have something to offer you through the experience of learning and personal growth.

I recently had the opportunity to be there for someone. When we talked on the phone, I could almost feel the desperation in their voice and knew they were at a point they felt there was no way out and did not know which way to turn. After we talked for a while, they realized that I was there for them and it was going to be alright, they let out a huge sigh and I could feel, through the phone, their relief.

I started to well up with emotion and pride that I was able to have the ability to ease the worry and pressure from this person as they are someone I love a great deal. This opportunity has happened many times with people I love. It is and will be some of the great achievements of my life.

This helps you reach a balance in your life that can be continued for years. And in the end, things must reach a balance. You need to have both given and received in order to feel that things are equal and fair. You have to receive in some way to avoid bitter and hateful feelings toward others. The average person can only give so much before they feel absolutely defeated and sucked dry by those around them. If you feel yourself heading in that direction, then you're due some quality 'me' time.

Take time out of your schedule to pamper yourself, to better your situation and to generally put yourself first. It will put you in a better position to help others later and will allow you to enjoy what you have worked for by developing a zest for life.

Without taking time out for yourself, you won't have anything to balance out your give, give, give nature. And if you don't take time to receive, be it giving to yourself or receiving from others, you may find yourself in the position of those you deal with where you are asking others to come to your rescue.

Your Vows to You

If I've done half as good a job making my argument, as I hope I have, then you're thinking of various ways to put yourself first in the back of your mind right now. If you should start down the road of healthy selfishness, as I hope you will, there will be people along the way who want to talk you out of it. They'll use guilt to get you to refocus on their needs and wants. They aren't going to understand what you're doing, how it stands to benefit them in the long run and they will do whatever they can to bring an end to it.

That's why you may need to keep a few key strategies in your mind to reference later when you face the various challenges you are bound to endure. I call it making vows to yourself because that's really what they are. You have to commit to bettering yourself and your circumstances before you can truly better anyone else's and it takes some headstrong, disciplined thinking to keep you on your way to achieving your goals.

• Be Strong

At some point, you will want to quit. It's inevitable. Someone will wear you down and force you to second-guess yourself. You will feel guilty about focusing on only yourself and bettering your own situation in life. You will face challenges so daunting that you would rather just go back to how it used to be. You may be a year into a master's degree or making strides toward a promotion at work or at least enjoying some of your past successes, and you will want to give it all up for various reasons, but you can't. You have to keep going in the face of all of these difficulties to achieve your full potential because the consequences of giving up are an unfulfilled, unhappy life. Early on, it was almost a daily occurrence for me that the thought of quitting would come into my mind. At those times I had to struggle, buckle down and forge ahead because I knew that quitting was not an option and I would have disastrous results if I gave in.

It's important in this case to remember to be strong and that this is something you've always wanted. You have to remember how much you wanted this when you first began and how it made so much sense to accomplish this goal in the first place. Your motivation to begin can help keep you going when things get tough. And they will get tough, so make this vow to yourself that you will be strong in spite of your many challenges. Your strength will be tested at some point, so keep the faith by believing in yourself. The end result will be worth the battle!

• Avoid People and Situations That Will Tempt You

You will face situations and have relationships that will test your desire to accomplish your goals. What we don't want to admit to ourselves is that we're weaker than we think when it comes to temptations. There is scientific research to back this up. A study that tested the will of smokers to resist the urge to light up a cigarette revealed that those who were the most confident about their self-control were the most likely to give into temptation. More than twice as many people who thought they could resist the urge to smoke eventually picked up a cigarette. Tests done using chocolate in place of cigarettes revealed similar results. Participants were routinely unable to successfully gauge the power of their urges.

This is something to keep in mind while you work to strengthen your relationship or put in extra time at work. Your urges are likely stronger than you anticipate and a good piece of advice to remember when temptation surfaces is to run the other direction- don't be overly confident in your ability to stand strong as that is the sure sign of great weakness. It's really that simple. By eliminating the opportunity to choose poorly, you also eliminate the possibility of committing that action. You may have the strength in time to fend off temptation, but for now it's best to master your strategies. Be strong in your resolve, but don't get cocky and ask for help or guidance when needed. Keep working and pamper yourself when it's necessary to recharge your batteries.

• Be Patient

Those around you won't understand when you go from helpful friend and family member to what may seem to them self-serving and self-absorbed. They may ask for your help and find that you turn them away when you used to always lend a helping hand. When you attempt to accomplish one of your major life goals, it will probably mean saying "no" more than a few times to family gatherings or other events that have been more important in the past. This may not sit well with some people, but you have to remind yourself that what you're doing will actually benefit everyone in the long run.

But more importantly than that, you have to remind yourself to be patient. Those people will come around in the end. You may find yourself making the same argument over and over endlessly, but it will sink in eventually. At some point, they will probably realize that maybe you really are going to make it, you really will improve your situation and ability to contribute and they should probably be helping you. But what you want to accomplish also won't happen overnight. It's going to take some time and effort, so don't get impatient. Everything – from understanding to success – will come in time.

• It's Not Always Easy, But It Is Simple

As you might understand, it's important for an addict or alcoholic to limit the time they spend with others who could trigger a relapse. That was the case with me when I was struggling to change my life. I found that it wasn't easy to change my routine of destructive behavior. Everyday brought opportunities to go back to my old way of living. Everyday brought a stressful situation that created a craving. What it takes isn't easy. It takes sacrifice, discipline and a reliance on your mentor and those who support you to achieve what you want. It's not something you have to go out and purchase. It's not something that has to be inherited. It's in each of us if we just want it bad enough. It's within us, it just takes work to get it out. Practice and it will eventually become a habit.

No matter what you want to accomplish in life, these same principles apply. But just because you may not have an addiction such as alcohol or drugs doesn't mean that this type of change is easy – but it is simple. Change for me meant not drinking or doing drugs, which is very simple. I was doing something destructive, so all I had to do was stop. It's a very simple task, but it took a lot out of me and a great deal of energy to sustain. It will probably be the same for you. If you want to start your own company, it's going to take courage to quit your job and accept that your future and income are uncertainties. It's not difficult to quit your job. Many of us have daydreamed about exactly how we'd like to do that. What is difficult is mustering the courage to do so and then face the challenges that arise.

This is true for just about every aspect of life. You need constant, unrelenting effort to do the little things it takes and the courage to begin the process. Quitting your job or destructive habits are simple concepts, but putting in the continuous, unrelenting effort to do those simple things require all you can give and if you are spread too thin emotionally to focus on what you really want, it will never happen and may even set you back considerably.

The Consequences of Selflessness

For those who don't regularly renew their own source of inner strength, the reasons can run the gamut. There are many people who as children were made to feel insignificant in some way. Giving of yourself can become a way to overcompensate for those insecurities. Sometimes this can cause individuals to be anxious, indecisive, neurotic and sensitive to criticism. They can strive for perfection in the worst way – by sacrificing their whole being.

Those who are capable of practicing healthy selfishness are peaceful, content and when they are faced with a problem, they meet it head-on and work actively to resolve it. They are realists who make decisions competently and confidently and accept criticism constructively. These people are not self-deniers who struggle and sacrifice for others out of guilt and feelings of unworthiness. Their needs and desires are acknowledged and resolved, not ignored and dismissed.

The consequence of selflessness without some kind of renewal or reward can be difficult. We find ourselves bone-tired yet unsatisfied with what we have been able to accomplish. We are still full of needs and wants that have not been met. We are left feeling as though others will give to us as we've given to them, but find instead that they are unable or unwilling to do so. We justify this behavior of others as an inability to contribute or repay and we tell ourselves that they don't see the pain they cause – thus justifying the emotions of betrayal. We try or pretend to put the hard feelings behind us and get on with our lives, but the bitterness and resentment festers.

Those who refuse to give to or empower themselves can eventually show signs of depression, feelings that they are over worked and underappreciated, impatience sprinkled with bouts of rage and unexplained tears.

The physiological implications are many as well. The stress of enduring someone else's burdens can leave you exhausted and suffering from headaches, sleeplessness and digestive problems.

The stress can result in higher levels of cortisol and insulin, which have been shown to damage arteries and lead to weight gain as the body's tendency to make and store fat strengthens. Stress can wear on bones, muscles and organs. It can lead to stroke, heart attacks and cancer.

When you give to others without ever receiving or taking time for yourself to rest and repair your body, you will unnecessarily stress yourself while wearing out your body - decreasing the likelihood of a long and healthy life. Exercising some selfishness may have a hugely positive impact on your life. With healthy selfishness you will feel unburdened and able to focus on what makes you happy. You may feel more energized and generally happier. You may be healthier physically as less stress reduces the strain and abuse your body suffers.

To undertake these attempts at major life changes, you have to learn to set boundaries with your various relationships. It's absolutely necessary, and as some would tell you, satisfying, to learn the incredibly important word, "No."

Learn to make decisions confidently and stick to them. When you say that you cannot help, stick to that response. You might be surprised at how much better you will feel.

The Power of No

Ask anyone who has consistently said "Yes" for a lifetime before finally saying "No" and they'll tell you how incredibly good it feels to finally do so. Not only does it have the positive health benefits already discussed, such as lowering stress and your risk of illness, but it also feels good to stand up for yourself. In order to confidently set and keep boundaries in your life, I've created a few tips and ideas to help.

1. Say "NO" correctly – Instead of simply saying "no" to a request, say, "No, because…" Simply saying "No" and offering no reason why just makes people think you're in a crabby mood. When you say no and give an honest reason as to why, people will probably understand. It's possible that they will be temporarily upset, but they will eventually understand. If your time is committed elsewhere and you're unable to help that person out of a jam, tell them why. "I have a big client presentation tomorrow, but maybe some other time." This is much better than a fabricated reason. People can generally see through fabricated excuses easily. If you're able to explain to them that you're attempting something that could change your life, they may be excited for you and forget that you're unable to help them at the moment. It could even inspire them to do the same.

Budgeting your time and knowing where and when you're committed is another great aid to saying "no." If you know you have to do X, Y, Z by Thursday, you know why you can't drop everything and help a friend finish his outdoor deck. It goes back to the honesty issue. Rather than being asked to do a favor and struggling to find a reason why you can't, a quick, "No, I can't, I'm doing this, this and this on Tuesday," is much more convincing than an unsure, "Well… I can't because…" and struggling to find your reason. This sounds like an excuse and it wouldn't if you tell them where you're needed and committed.

Try saying "yes." I know, it sounds crazy, but if someone asks you to help them finish their deck this weekend, say yes, but request that it be done later because you're booked up. If they are up against a deadline (such as the in-laws are visiting this weekend) and you're unable to help them prior to that time, then they will be forced to go elsewhere for help. By putting off the favor because you're busy, they may also want to avoid burdening you and find another solution on their own. It may also help to put the ball back in their court by asking that they first complete a list of actions. "Get all of the plans and materials, level the area, dig the post holes and mark off the dimensions. Let me know when you're ready and we'll set up a weekend next month to complete it." Put the onus on them to take action before you ever undertake the task. This option should only be used if you are serious about helping them later should they fulfill all of the obligations you ask.

"I'd love to but..." is another phrase you should commit to memory. It's polite because you are eager to help and interested in the task, but isn't a flat "no." You can follow this up with helpful alternatives or other ideas to accomplish the end goal without being directly involved. For instance, you can suggest another friend who is much more experienced in building a deck than you and who has more time to help. This allows you to gracefully bow out, while offering them an even better alternative.

You can also take a pre-emptive strike approach in an indirect way. If your friend tells you that they have purchased a house and you can sense that they will soon ask you for help moving, mention that you wish you could see the place, but you're so booked up for the next month you can hardly breathe. If you can't even *look* at the new house, they'll know that you surely don't have the time to help them move into it. You have declined the offer before they ever had a chance to ask and you avoid the situation altogether.

Finally, mix and match your strategies. When a friend calls to talk to you with their deck, politely decline to help before they ask while putting the ball back in their court and suggesting an alternative. "I've been so busy that I couldn't even hang a door on an outhouse this year but I know Ron just finished a great deck up at his cottage on the lake, I'm sure he'd have some great advice for you." Or with the friend who needs help moving, "Your house sounds great. My mom used a great moving company when she sold her home. You should give me a call back in a few days, and I'll get that company's name for you."

There are many ways to say "no," but the outcome is really what you are after. You want to lessen your load while encouraging others to be more self-sufficient. It's not that you can't or shouldn't help on occasion, you just have to be aware not to sacrifice your long term goals for someone else's immediate wants or needs. Once you have created more space and time in your life, you can use that time to really focus on you and what will help you reach your goals. Taking care of your own mental and emotional health as well as lowering your stress level gives rise to tremendous creativity.

Now don't think that I'm perfect at this all the time. I still tend to overload myself on occasion and this happened just recently. I was going through one of those stretches where business was booming. I had new clients and then some old clients who were all needing things from me. At the same time, I was scheduled to go off on a family vacation for a little over a week to Cuba. I really looked forward to this vacation to be with a large group of friends and family and enjoy some time away. I could have let the fact that I was buried at work keep me from going – or even keep me from fully enjoying my time away, but I refused to allow it. I went and fully enjoyed myself getting the chance to catch up with everyone and lay around in the sun. It was a time of reconnection with those I loved and renewal for myself.

Instead of feeling guilty or like I should be somewhere else, I instead felt energized and ready to dig back into business when I got back. I chose to carve out time for myself and I think actually did a better job for my clients when I returned because I was rested and had a renewed energy. We've probably all had the experience of being so tired we can even think, but you don't have to work around the clock or get less sleep to fit everything in. This is an indicator that your life has become less about what you want and more about those thousand things that drain your time and energy. Instead, you must prioritize your tasks and choose to make time for you as a person to reconnect with those things that renew your heart and soul.

Charles Whyte

Chapter 8
The Mouse Trap

Charles Whyte

Chapter 8
The Mouse Trap

Perhaps you have already planned and set in motion a long-term goal to get yourself in a healthy and stable situation to set yourself up for success. This long-term plan will contain hundreds, if not thousands, of opportunities to make a mistake or be faced with unforeseen challenges. It's inevitable that at some point you are going to misstep and find yourself scrambling to recover, or worse, considering giving up completely. The idea is not to prevent every mistake or to try to be perfect, but rather to understand that life is a 'learn as you go' process and these challenges are merely pointing you in a better direction. It is your choice how you handle each obstacle you encounter and those decisions will determine if you succeed or choose to give up.

A good example I heard recently is of a young man named Wade. Wade recently bought a home in hopes of flipping it for a healthy profit. It's a very common moneymaking strategy, though it not without its risks. Wade chose what he thought was the perfect fixer-upper and, once purchased, started selected demolition of the areas to be upgraded. As the walls revealed their secrets, Wade noticed many do-it-yourself specials within the home – poorly done wiring, substandard materials and no regard for city code. Wade quickly realized he'd uncovered more work than he'd anticipated, which had the potential to cut deeply into his profits. He had a decision to make. Do the right thing and correct the problems or cover it up and make a bigger profit. Wade decided to just put up new sheetrock and painted it without making the necessary repairs and later sold the house for a profit.

The new family who purchased the home soon makes the same discoveries as Wade did while making their own improvements. Because they can tell new sheetrock from the original materials used to erect the wall, they know that the seller uncovered the code violations and simply covered them back up, exposing them to potential fire risk and the expense of correcting the issues.

The family takes legal action against Wade, and in the end, he suffers a big financial hit. Wade has encountered quite a setback and he has two ways to deal with it moving forward. He can take responsibility for his actions and evaluate what he can do better next time, or he can quit. It would be easy for him to think, "Well I got a dud of a house so it's not my fault," but that wouldn't address the real issue. The real issue is that when confronted with the first challenge of problems that should be fixed, Wade took the easy way out and made even more problems for himself later on.

Some errors in judgment are normal, especially if you are entering an area of endeavor that you are unfamiliar with. The important issue is how you react and how you let those errors influence how you proceed. If you become too afraid of making an error to try again, then you have lost your objectivity of the bigger picture. This is true in business endeavors or even personal endeavors.

Blue Jean Millionaire

I know a friend named Steve who, several years ago, went through some terrible financial troubles, eventually culminating in bankruptcy. It seemed that his entire life fell apart as over a two month period. His wife moved out and asked for a divorce, leaving him with a young child to care for by himself. Steve used to say that the only thing that didn't happen to him during this time was that his dog didn't die! It was almost like the lyrics to a bad country song.

Within a few years however, Steve was back on his feet and had met someone new. His daughter was doing well and he had started his own business. It was a struggle, but now he had a partner in life so he worked hard at it. Then suddenly he was injured again on the job, but being the owner, he had no income for many months and even with his wife's income he was once again in desperate financial straits.

It was at this point that Steve and I had a real in-depth discussion. We all have circumstances in our lives that occur on occasion. But when you have episodes in your life that seem to repeat a pattern, it's time to admit that the source of the problem isn't 'them', it's you. Steve was so fearful that he would repeat that terrible time in his life, he began questioning and blaming everything else in his life. So rather than looking for solutions, he started a downward spiral that again devastated his life. As his attitude got worse, more problems piled on and he continued to choose poorly allowing them to be his downfall.

I've seen this frequently with people who have relationship problems, health issues and even addictions. They seem to think that one small challenge or misstep wipes out all the work they've accomplished and so there's no use in trying. This brings about worse results than they can even imagine and digs a deep hole they sometimes can't see a way out of. I have fallen into this trap myself a time or two.

Failure is truly a state of mind. There is no reason to allow a mistake to cripple you, your business and your ability to make a living because you have the power to change your perception of these challenges as you go. Given the vast number of opportunities there are to err in your life, challenges and mistakes aren't optional – they are inevitable. Decide right now how you will meet those challenges and what motivation you will give yourself to find solutions and move past the roadblocks.

Common Pitfalls

While a great many mistakes are made as a direct result of decisions that we make, some are not. It's true that events just happen. Those troubles that arise through no fault of our own are sometimes the hardest to deal with, such as Steve's wife walking out on him and leaving him to juggle a young child and job alone with no notice. Events such as this have the potential to make us feel so victimized and so unfairly treated that it's hard to muster the motivation to deal with them. There are also situations with relationships that can destroy your positive outlook and make it very difficult to move forward. But move forward you must, as I had to.

Personal Relationships

I would be the first to say that personal relationships can be tough. Arguments with your spouse or a close friend or relative can leave you feeling bitter and resentful – and that feeling is hard to leave at home. You bring those feelings and distractions with you to the workplace and allow them to affect your performance. This can show itself in a number of ways. You could be impatient with clients and customers, short with coworkers and can even snap at supervisors. You may also be noticeably depressed, tearful, distracted and disinterested in your duties.

I have experienced divorce and it was a devastating experience. I was emotionally drained and financially battered by the whole dissolution of the marriage which dragged out for months. Yes it severely affected my ability to perform professionally and my income suffered as well. When this sort of life altering scenario is happening in your life it can really be the perfect storm of events that have the possibility to ruin your life.

After my wife told me she wasn't in love with me any more, I acted strong and as if I was all right, but inside I was destroyed. I felt like after all this time and work there was a chance for me once again to have that white picket fence and happy contented life with a partner who loved me and would be by my side. I would have moments where I would break down and cry and feel hopeless. I felt like I could not battle for that life again and face the risk of losing again. It affected my work as I felt as if I'd lost my motivation and that no one cared anyway. But then I remembered the 'cat and mouse' incident and started to get a little angry with myself. I knew I had to fight my way out of the pit. But here again, you have a choice. You can sit back in your bitterness and rage and allow those emotions to consume you, or you can choose to keep going. Is it easy? No. In fact it was one of the hardest things I've ever gone through and I did it by putting my head down and focusing on what I really wanted. I had the support and encouragement of many, family and friends, and they were great when I chose to seek their counsel. I wanted to be financially sound again. I wanted to pay off a mortgage I was stuck with after the divorce. I wanted to have a little cottage in the woods that would be my refuge.

There is no easy way out of this type of traumatic situation but to motivate yourself to keep you mind on the end result. Had I focused on the piles of bills, the money that was going out the window to pay for the divorce or the fact that what

I'd worked for all those years was torn apart, I might not have ever made it. Instead I focused on each day – and some days on each hour – doing what I could do. I focused on the small victories no matter how small. I could work. I could refuse to wallow in self pity. I could ask for help from others and get ideas to help me move farther faster. I could spend time with positive energetic people that loved me rather than becoming a bitter recluse.

Relationships are hard, but they can also be a positive motivator if you refuse to cut yourself off from those you love and who want to support you. In time, I realized I had grown through all the negative experiences and was much stronger, but it was tough for a while. If you are in a similar situation, hang in there and you will come out a better person for having weathered the storm.

Health Issues

Illness and injury can really stall your attempts to establish a firm financial foundation. I know a Harley enthusiast named Tommy who has quite a story to tell about finances and personal injury. Tommy had a reputation for moving around a lot, never being satisfied with his current situation and displaying more than a few maturity issues. After switching jobs yet again in an unstable, tumultuous life, Tommy opted out of some optional short-term disability coverage provided by his new employer. One day while leaving work on his motorcycle in a light rain, the bike's back tire slipped and he was thrown from the motorcycle. The tumble dislocated his shoulder and left Tommy out of work and with no disability or insurance coverage.

It took three months of zero income and recovery time before he could return to work as a surgical tech. Tommy and his wife fell behind on bills and ultimately filed for bankruptcy. This was devastating, but Tommy's response was a positive one. He struggled, but he never gave up. He came within an inch of losing his home and surely endured significant marital troubles while going through such a tough financial period. But he kept his house, came through the bankruptcy and is making a comfortable living today. As I stated, I too had lengthy periods where my income was reduced due to medical issues and these type of things just happen sometimes.

There are numerous times when you might have a physical, or even emotional, challenge that you must overcome. Maybe it is a chronic condition such as diabetes, or excess weight or even a simple lack of exercise. There can also be the unexpected medical events such as Tommy experienced.

Again, it is the way you approach these events that determines your outcome, not the fact that they happen. I knew I had to keep going through the rough spots when this happened to me because not only was my financial future at stake, so was my quality of life. I can say now that it was definitely worth it though it was difficult at times. Its times like this that I have to remind myself why I am doing this. My reason is important and has kept me going many a time when it would have been so much easier to quit.

Some of the most difficult health related problems to overcome are those you bring on yourself such as a bad habit like smoking, or obesity. These habits not only shorten your life, but they decrease your productivity and ability to do more. Being successful isn't about pushing yourself to the limit. It's also about taking the time to care for what you need physically to enable you to respond the best way possible when challenges arise.

Lack of Commitment

A simple lack of commitment is something that you control, which can also needlessly complicate your situation. It's my own personal belief that what we have to do in order to get on firm financial ground isn't difficult and it doesn't take any high level of intelligence. What it does take is the work ethic and motivation to do those simple tasks day-in and day-out to establish yourself and create the life you want. That's the hard part. It takes work every day, or at least all the days that end in "y"! Even when things aren't going well, that motivation has to be there to keep going.

Those who rely on making sales for their income, as I have for most of my life, go through dry spells where every call and every sales opportunity turn up nothing. A start-up business may take years to become profitable. Becoming a highly educated professional may take years of study and scraping by before you see any return. Those are the times that really test your level of commitment. A lack of commitment will devastate any chance of successfully accomplishing any major goal, so you have to push through those times. You must decide what has to be done and then do it.

After years of living in a cycle of working hard and coasting, working hard and coasting, I know from experience that you can't just avoid those things that need to be done. I really struggled, both professionally and in married life, because of this pattern of thinking. You absolutely cannot get things moving in the right direction and then put it on autopilot and expect to have a great outcome. Just like an airplane on autopilot will eventually crash without some time and attention, areas of business or personal life will as well. This is a sneaky little habit that interferes with my progress from time to time. I have to be ever vigilant of coasting through life even to this day.

Cynicism

We've all heard about those offers and opportunities that come along that are too good to be true. Exercising a little cynicism isn't always a bad thing when it comes to ridiculous claims of success and wealth. Conventional wisdom says that when someone approaches you with an investment or opportunity that sounds too good to be true, it usually is. The easiest and most obvious example of this are those employment listings that allow you to work from home and earn $1,000 per week. They say you can earn $50,000 annually by taking surveys, you don't need any experience, and so on. These descriptions send up red flags with most people, and for good reason. These "opportunities" are not opportunities at all but rather an enticement to spend more money purchasing a program.

If you've fallen into one of these situations in the past, and felt taken advantage of, it's possible that you're now hyper-vigilant about "scams" and supposed great opportunities. However, it's also important that you not handicap yourself by assuming everything is a scam. This means that you are too afraid of your own judgment to evaluate a situation and make a good decision. It is important to trust your instincts and evaluate opportunities, and people, objectively. Make your decisions based on the intimate knowledge of your abilities, strengths and weaknesses. You know what you are capable of and what you aren't, so proceed with that knowledge.

Making good decisions is about understanding the balance between cynicism and blind trust. You must give yourself the opportunity to learn and understand that there will be times when learning is quite hard, but it is a necessary part of the process. Unfortunately, we often grow the most when we learn a hard lesson but we must be vigilant that this lesson doesn't stop the flow of success completely.

Deal with it

It would be great if we could crawl under a rock when we make mistakes, but we have to deal with our problems – and will – regardless of whether or not we choose to make the best of them. When we make mistakes in our professional or personal lives, it's always best to just deal with the problem with a healthy attitude and to carry the process through to the end rather than retreat to our comfort zones. Once we find our way back to that comfort zone we all have, it takes a great deal of motivation and energy to get things moving again once you've allowed them to cease. After all, it takes more energy to get an object moving than it does to keep it moving.

If what you're doing isn't working, *it isn't working*. Someone is trying to tell you something. Change is in order. For whatever reason things aren't working out, maybe a lack of commitment set you back or a divorce distracted you from your responsibilities, you have to change what you're doing. You might be turned off by the risk involved in making changes but there is more danger in going down a path you know is a dead end rather than at least trying to make things better.

Risk is a necessary part of the process to succeed. It's not those that do as everyone else is doing that stand out, that may live a comfortable yet average life. It's the individuals who don't concern themselves with what others think who accomplish the most. It's the individuals who aren't afraid to stretch the boundaries who live a fulfilled life. It's the individuals who venture into unknown territory and accept the risk involved who end up living with financial freedom.

Bad business decisions, bouts of laziness, injury, illness, divorce – they can all be overcome. Changing your habits, being creative and willingly accepting the unknown can turn your life around. Just get started, even a small beginning is something to build on.

Forgive Yourself

Forgiveness of oneself is vital to recovery in any area of life. Everyone is going to make mistakes, so don't be too hard on yourself when you make one. Too often we have a tendency to blame ourselves more harshly than we would others. Some of us think that we have to hold onto those feelings and harsh criticisms of ourselves so that we make sure we've learned from our mistakes. What we really do with our constant remembrance of mistakes is build a wall between ourselves and our future. But forgiveness does not mean forgetting. Forgiveness allows us to let go of the negative and damaging emotions while continuing on the path to success.

Forgiveness does not mean that you are weak or don't have the courage to face your mistakes. It means that you have acknowledged them and you are attempting to move past them by choosing courage and strength rather than turning yourself into a victim of your own negative feelings. I have made my share of mistakes and the people who matter have forgiven me. If they can, then I must forgive others also, and have. This way I have moved forward to have a fulfilling life. Remember: those that mind don't matter and those that matter, don't mind. You are one of those that matter.

The reason we have this guilt and shame over making mistakes is a high level of pride. Many people hold themselves to ridiculously high standards setting up their own failure in their mind before they even try something new. They take the attitude that nothing they do is ever good enough and eventually, this is translated in a reluctance to try anything new. Pride is thinking of ourselves as being wiser, more insightful, even intuitive and therefore beyond making mistakes. It's a fundamentally flawed way of thinking and is going to act only to hurt us at some point. Acknowledge your pride, and more importantly, acknowledge that it is destructive.

Failing to forgive yourself will only help you to hurt others. It's a fact that hurting people have a tendency to hurt others. Addicts are a perfect example of this. They are so pained inside that they escape reality through drug use. And when they abuse drugs, it's their friends and family who suffer the most.

They lose the person who is so important to them. Relationships crumble and bitter feelings follow when an addict consistently checks out of reality because it's just too painful while friends and family are left to deal with it. When that addiction grows unchecked, it will devour every part of the addict's life, and no good can come of that. The hurt feelings you harbor will make you quicker to anger, and the more explosive you become, the more likely you are to disrupt relationships and hurt others. Forgive yourself, just as I learned to, because you have nothing to lose and everything to gain.

Move On

Unfortunately, there are no reset buttons in the real world. Mistakes happen and they must be resolved. You really have no choice but to handle them and do your best to move on. When you don't allow yourself to just let it go, you lug around excess baggage that ties you down and, at best, severely slows your progress. At worst, you're stuck in that stage where you know you've made a mistake and can't move on because it would just be too difficult to do so.

We "just get over it" by focusing on new goals and activities. A child who makes a poor test grade probably doesn't stand a good chance of having the teacher change that grade. This child will likely only progress if they shift their focus to the next test and vow to perform better. It's a constructive and healthy thought process to admit that you could have done better, but also to have to correct it later on. What's done is done, and it's difficult to fully grasp this concept as simple as it is. Even as adults, we feel the need to go back and correct, but in a lot of situations, the only thing we can do is apply the lessons learned to future endeavors. It is what it is.

Even hearing and believing that hanging onto negative past experiences serve no purpose in our lives doesn't necessarily help us to let go of those experiences. Do past mistakes help you moving forward? Do they work in your favor in any conceivable way? Let go of those feelings and focus on future goals. When you focus on the future and what is possible, you are choosing a healthy perspective over a destructive perspective. And focusing on the positive will attract the positive.

Relax

Even when we make mistakes, what we lose touch with is that we are attempting to better our lives. We are moving in the right direction even though we may have taken steps backward along the way. When you strive to improve your life and you're making decisions with that final goal in mind, *it's a good thing*. When I think about it, what I've done in making and then recovering from mistakes in my life, is enable myself to help others. You can't sit up on a mount in white robes telling people how to live and expect to really help them. They will assume you have no idea how to live in the real world and will not hear anything you have to say.

As I look back over all the good experiences in my life (there have been many!) and the few hard lessons I had to learn over the course of the last five decades, I can see that those mistakes and errors where leading me to place when I can honestly tell someone how to improve their life. I have been there myself and because I have that practical real world experience, I can definitely help you skip over a pothole or two!

So relax and don't take yourself so seriously. If you're able to laugh at yourself from time to time, then you have a relaxed and healthy outlook. I laugh at myself all the time and it relieves the stress and allows me to see other options. Your attempts to get yourself on firm financial footing shouldn't be so stodgy and buttoned-up that you can never laugh, never make a mistake and never get over things. Have you ever noticed how being focused on not getting hurt will likely result in getting hurt? When we tense up to avoid pain, that's when we seem to suffer the most of it.

By taking things less seriously and just remembering that this is all part of a positive plan for our lives, we're better able to enjoy it and accept the challenges associated with it. Focus on the future, what you can accomplish and how exciting all of that is.

Chapter 9
Starting Over

Charles Whyte

Chapter 9

Starting Over

Starting over can seem so big and impossible, while at the same time it can be exciting and energizing. I know for me it was both dependent on the day, hour, minute or sometimes even second. Climbing out of your 'pit' can take all you have to give at times. I know for me it did, but it was definitely worth it. While it seems that your 'pit' is endless, there are always options to dig out. Let's look at some companies who did just that.

Circuit City, up until recently, was the second largest electronics retailer. You probably heard about the great deal of financial troubles the company had leading up to 2009. The company, in September 2008, reported a loss of over $230 million. That's an astounding amount of money to lose. More surprising is the fact that that loss represents only a quarter of the company's fiscal year.

Circuit City's failures were plentiful. During the '80's and 90s, many believe that the company relaxed when it should have been purchasing real estate in key locations. When they settled for out-of-the-way locations, they lost a great deal of business to many other large retailers. The company also regressed by discontinuing the sale of appliances which was responsible for a large percentage of their sales. Along with some failed ventures and choosing not to heavily promote Apple products, the company made many more managerial mistakes that are widely accepted as reasons that it closed its doors in early 2009.

If you think more than a quarter of a billion dollars is a lot of money to lose in a quarter, video game producer Sega Corp. reported losses of approximately $472.9 million for a 12-month period in the early 2000's. For those that struggle financially, it's hard to fathom losing half a billion dollars in one year or a quarter of a million dollars in just three months. But it happened and will happen again. Those companies turned in enormous losses and guess what. They're still going today.

Much was made of Circuit City closing its doors. The economy and the fervor about how it's the worst recession since the great depression made bankruptcies big news. In a time when record job losses, unemployment benefit claims and bankruptcies are the sought-after stories of the day, the comeback stories are sometimes ignored. But just like Sega did nearly a decade ago, Circuit City came back, albeit slimmer in its new form, as an online store selling many of the products it had on its shelves the previous year.

Even when financial ruin looks unavoidable, the companies that are resilient and have headstrong management can always keep the company functioning, turning a profit to avoid complete collapse.

No one would think twice if Circuit City closed its doors and ceased to function in any capacity ever again. That's because it's so easy to quit when you're faced with financial ruin. When you're in a million dollar hole, no one expects you to climb out. Ever. But it happens all the time. Those who go bankrupt, face foreclosure, fall into debt up to their neck, can turn things around more often than you are probably aware of.

As with everything, the media tends to focus on bad news so when someone, or some company, makes a big turnaround no one ever hears about it. People you are around each day are probably the same way. All they seem to talk about is how hard things are, how impossible it is to get ahead and how silly it is to even try. You must have enough courage of conviction to believe that you are right and they are wrong. The thing I had to be real sure of and keep myself convinced of *all the time* is that I was right and would get back up no matter the setbacks.

You may be one of the unfortunate few who face a complete financial meltdown as you effort toward your own personal goal, so I feel compelled to tell you that there is nothing that cannot be beaten. Here again, I've been there more than once wondering how in the world I was going to improve my situation. It doesn't matter if a business partner takes you and your finances for a ride, if you suffer a devastating injury that leaves you unable to pay bills or even work, regardless of why you're in need of financial recovery, just know it *is* possible.

I was living at my Dad's house, feeling defeated when I had my 'cat and mouse' moment. From then on, I visualized my own house in a nice, desirable area. I had many setbacks to the point I almost allowed myself to think it might not happen, but I would just set my jaw and stubbornly say NO! I forged ahead and kept my dream alive. It worked and today I live in a very nice house in a very nice area. I really believe this is in great part to seeing it and continuing to believe it would happen.

Focus is key. It's key as you build a vehicle for recovery, whether that means getting a degree or starting a company or climbing the ladder within an existing company, just as it is when you are devastated by a loss. Focus has several synonyms. Motivation, concentration, center of attention – they are all interchangeable. Financial ruin requires you to put your full efforts into recovery. Failing to make your recovery, whatever that means to you specifically, is not an option. Your focus is like trying to start a company in your spare time, when you feel like getting around to it. That doesn't sound like someone motivated to start a company, and it doesn't sound like someone who ever will start a company. You aren't going to accidentally create a business. It takes your attention and a motivation that drives you to actively think about and take steps toward making it a reality.

The same can be said for your financial recovery. It's not going to happen overnight and it's not going to happen by itself. Think about your recovery, what it will take to make it happen and force yourself to take the necessary steps in the process. It's not easy to file for bankruptcy, but sometimes that's what it takes to keep your business going or keep your family in a home. We have to make sacrifices like, to a degree, admitting defeat and starting over. I had to do this myself, but once you make that decision, it's like getting a clean slate to start over. It's scary, but exciting too.

Remember where you wanted to go when you started. I can guarantee you it wasn't a homeless shelter, so don't accept that as a possible outcome. You had grand plans and hopes for yourself from the onset, and you shouldn't lose sight of those or water them down to something "more realistic." Visualizing your dreams coming true is an actual theory that some would swear by, and it can help you accomplish your goals even if you're starting over.

Jim Carrey once wrote himself a $10 million check – years before he was a successful actor – as a motivation tool. He wanted to someday cash that check to himself. Basketball great Michael Jordan used to visualize his shot going in before he ever took it. These techniques of seeing what you want happening are a way of motivating you to work toward accomplishing them. It's the basis of the Law of Attraction and *The Secret*, a book and movie based on the belief. While work is definitely a step of the recovery process, we have to first know what we're working toward. Remembering your original goal and visualizing how you will make it a reality will allow you to identify what specific steps have to be taken to accomplish that. As I have told myself so many times, quitting is not an option. It will not get the job done.

There's No Such Thing

You and your family are traveling by car on an isolated, winding stretch of road through vast wilderness. You're on your way to a secluded cottage to spend a relaxing week away from the demands of everyday life. Imagine you run out of gas as you reach the midway point between the main road and your vacation spot. By foot, you are hours away from either destination. What do you do?

If your attempt at achieving a life of financial freedom fails, you're in much the same position. You cannot quit. In this case, there is no such thing. You can't drive your car until it sputters its last ounce of gasoline and then give up. Admitting defeat will not put gas in the tank just like quitting on your dreams will not rescue you from financial hardship. You are in a situation and have to deal with it. If your car sputtered to a stop in the road on your family vacation, no one would cancel the vacation. And even if you wanted to cancel the vacation, that would not magically put a full tank of gas in your car either. I know for me there were times ignoring my problems was comfortable and I like to feel comfortable. I now know that real change and growth can sometimes be uncomfortable and tough to face, but face it I did.

Finding yourself amid financial ruin is much the same. Admitting mistakes or saying you failed is not going to instantly and effortlessly fix things. It takes reassessing your course, changing your plan of action and adjusting to your new situation to still meet your final goals. "I quit," is a meaningless phrase that you can say to everyone that will be heard by no one.

Sometimes we think that we can ignore our problems and they will go away. But when we realistically look at our situation, we know that that's far from reality. When given the opportunity to ignore our problems, however, it's easy to justify. We can escape in a night of drinking, lose ourselves in television, retreat to activities with family and friends, but none of these actions (or lack of action) solves anything. The problems remain while we busy ourselves with other people and activities and are likely to compound rather than go away while we avoid them. Debts accumulate interest, those to whom you owe money or services become angry, debt collectors take steps to repossess and your credit score goes lower, lower, lower. Shop all you like, watch all the movies you like, eat, drink, sleep the day away, and your problems fester all the while. They don't understand the words, "I quit." A best case scenario as you avoid your financial problems is that they will remain there, unchanged – and that's the best case.

The likely outcome, however, is that problems give way to more problems if they are not properly handled. Money problems can't be paused while you work up the courage and motivation to handle them. There is no "in between" handling a problem and allowing it to get worse. You deal with a problem or you likely allow it to get worse. Inaction is not an option.

If you find that the business you started is unable to pay its debts, isn't profitable and you're going to lose your home if you don't start bringing home a paycheck, you're probably reaching a crisis point that will force you to quit or take some other drastic measure to avoid collapse. Even if you feel quitting is an option for you, what are you quitting to do? Are you quitting to join the pool of available employees? Are quitting to hopefully find work elsewhere? If you quit you must start over again which is harder than fixing the problems you have now.

I'm reminded of a friend, Jon, who recently joined the job market. His previous position was vice president of operations for a publishing company. Jon, despite having only a year of college, had worked in publishing for more than ten years moving up rapidly and recently earned approximately $100,000 per year. There was a strained relationship with a supervisor in the company that eventually led to Jon's position being "eliminated." Jon harbored a great deal of bitterness and resentment and found it frustrating that he could be pushed aside so easily.

Jon tried to find work elsewhere, but was unable to. Showing a high-ranking position within a well-established company and earning such good money made Jon an intimidating hire. But that wasn't the biggest issue. Jon was insecure about his lack of education and soon became convinced that no one would hire him in a position equivalent to the one he had left. He constantly perused the want ads for jobs that paid $30,000-$50,000. Why would someone who made $100,000 a year ago want to earn $30,000? Why would someone who wielded such power as recently as a few months ago want to take on such a limited, non-managerial role now?

The answer is that he only believed himself to be worth that lower amount. He had low self-esteem and was convinced no one would consider his experience that valuable. As a result, he was forcing himself to start completely over at the bottom of the pay scale rather than just keep going from where he was. Amazingly, people do this to themselves all the time. Rather than pick up where they left off and use all the knowledge they have gained, they take several steps backward.

Don't get me wrong, everyone gets worn down and frustrated sometimes when it feels that you can't keep going. But recognize this is a temporary emotion and not one you can base long term decisions on. Quitting on yourself, your business, your progress and what you've learned will not be the answer that you thought it was. Walking away may leave you with those same debts and stressors, but with the added difficulty of recreating your life. You're just as likely to get your business or your career back on the right track by simply sticking with it and pushing through your difficult time.

What I've found is that if there is anything that you should quit doing, it's complaining about your situation. Focusing on all the negative just makes things worse, as Jon discovered. He was so bitter and angry about being let go from his former employer that he couldn't fully concentrate on moving forward.

If your business or venture is struggling along with the economy, I have news for you. Everyone's struggling. You can complain, whine and seek the pity of others, but what good does that do for your situation? Life happens. That's a fact that will never change, and no amount of complaining will change that. When negative events happen in your life, you can complain about them or you can get focused and do something about it.

My own experiences have taught me that the latter is much more productive. I have found many times in my life that just being positive has beneficial effects. "Fake it 'til you make it!" By this I don't mean being phony, I mean really try hard to be positive and polite and you will be amazed how much better it makes you feel and that you actually do become positive. People start to notice you are always happy and want to be around you. They want to work with you and help you. By choosing to present yourself as happy, you can make that happiness a reality.

Two Steps Forward and Three Steps Back

There are those times when you are devastated in your professional or personal life by some circumstance and its vital that you react in a healthy, appropriate manner. Instead of complaining and looking for someone else to solve your problem while you run and hide, you choose to work toward a solution. You make a plan and begin working right away to set things right. Instead of resolving your situation, however, you find that all the work you've done has only set you back even more.

Struggling with addiction like I did presents you with a lot of opportunities to work hard only to have it all undone with one mistake. I would work hard on my sobriety, work to repair personal relationships and do my best to provide stability for my family only to have it all taken away by slipping back into my old habits or by responding in a less than healthy way to a given event. My wife and I worked in a printing plant, and struggled for a few years to keep those jobs while we paid down old debts. Our plan, which included the tried and true option of robbing Peter to pay Paul, eventually unraveled when we learned that Peter wasn't all that reliable and we were really just treading water. It was obviously a poor plan, but we really worked hard during that time only to have things eventually come apart. But I still knew success was in my future so I refocused and started in again with a new plan

In times when we bust our butts to fix what we've done to our lives, a plan – and, learn from my mistake here, a *good* plan – is the first thing we need to take the steps toward freedom. Without a clear plan of action, we're just running around completing random, unrelated tasks with only a vague idea of what you want to ultimately accomplish. If you want to pay off a big credit card debt for example, think of random money-generating ideas like doing some consulting work on the side or perhaps a part time job. Maybe you can simply de-clutter your life and sell those unwanted items in a yard sale or on EBay. As you take small actions to change your life, you will find that more ideas flow through you. Taking action feels good and having a plan, even a small one, always gave me a sense of direction and some peace of mind because I could focus on that goal and not get distracted by the other things going on in my life.

Devise a clear plan that can tell you approximately how long it will take to meet your goals and what it involves. The person with credit card debt, we'll call him Jeremy, might decide to wait tables on the weekend. Because Jeremy has a waiter friend who can get him a job at his restaurant and can tell him what to expect in the way of tips from the clientele, he knows that he will bring in about $200-$300 per weekend. And if he couples that with swapping restaurant outings with trips to the grocery store and picking up the occasional weekday evening shift, he plans on having an additional $1,400 per month, conservatively, to pay down his debt. With that information, he knows that it will take him approximately 6 months to pay off his credit card – and that's if he doesn't find other ways to cut his expenses.

This is a good plan because it tells Jeremy how long it will take to complete his objective and involves real sacrifice that he knows up front. What you're going to find is that if what you want to accomplish is worth attempting, it's going to involve sacrifice. Jeremy is going to be sacrificing a lot to accomplish his goal of paying off his credit card debt. He won't have a weekend to himself for roughly 6 months – but the outcome is worth it to him. You might imagine that another key part of recovery is sticking to the plan you devised. There will be times when Jeremy is bone tired and will want to quit, but he has to have the stick-to-itiveness to resolve his debt. We won't go anywhere or accomplish anything if we bail on our goals when things make us tired or frustrated or stressed.

Jeremy, by sacrificing and working hard throughout his plan, may find that he spent more on restaurant dining than he thought and could save $250 per month by learning to cook a few meals. He may discover that he is capable of avoiding those impulse purchases that end up costing him so much money. He may find that he can continue living his more cost efficient lifestyle beyond the 6-month period, which will afford him the ability to start and contribute to a retirement or investment account. This may mean an earlier retirement full of travel and enjoyment as opposed to a late, cash-strapped retirement. While no one expects Jeremy to go without days off until his retirement, the small steps he took in cutting out unnecessary costs could teach him how a little less now means a lot more later. That's going to hold true for you too. Small steps now can definitely mean great leaps toward the life you really want.

When I ran into financial troubles, it was turning the big deficit into small, doable daily tasks that kept me focused and gave the feeling I was constantly making progress every day. I sat down with pen and paper, mapped out how much I needed to pay each month and devised a way to meet that goal. As I met these small goals, I further broke down the big goals into even easier steps and was able to accelerate my income way beyond what I needed to make ends meet. I found that it's the little actions that chip away at your tasks until they crumble, not necessarily the big events.

Lean on Me

It always helps to have friends to lean on in times of need as well. A study published in the Journal of Experimental Social Psychology told an interesting story about the importance of friendship. A group of people were placed at the bottom of a steep hill with a heavy backpack and asked to judge the steepness of the hill. The study focused on whether or not the physiological resource of social support affected the visual perception of a slope. The result of the study was that those who had a friend alongside for the study judged the slope of the hill to be less extreme than those who were alone. It's a powerful example of the importance of friendship and a social network when faced with challenges.

A resourceful and strong network of friends will not only be there for emotional support in tough times, but can also help you along the way in more direct ways. A supportive friend can help you financially through tough times or may mentor you if you are starting into a new unfamiliar area. They are a source of information and can provide you with resources you need to focus on moving forward.

Believe that you can do it. Even when it seems like everything you try leads to more problems, keep opening doors. One of them, at some point, is going to be the one that affords you the life you're looking for. Each step of the process toward recovery has the potential to give way to a wave of momentum and success.

Put the blinders on and just get it done. When my second marriage ended, I was faced with some difficult financial hurdles. I had to take out a second mortgage on the home, but I found that putting the blinders on really helped me. I focused on nothing but the task at hand, on making money and on repairing my finances. I had a job, invested heavily and gave some other sources of income the appropriate attention to take off. Because I put the past in the past, devised a plan to recover financially and worked my tail off, I was able to pay off a 6-digit mortgage in four years. It was a lot of work and I had to stay focused on the reasons why. But I got it done.

Is it great being mortgage free? You bet! I'm proof that it can be done and so can you. Believe.

Charles Whyte

Chapter 10
House of Power

Chapter 10

House of Power

It was a long climb up from addiction and financial struggles to, finally, financial freedom. I took my lumps along the way, that's for sure. I sewed holes closed in my socks because I couldn't afford to replace them. When I had no money to offer, I traded my work for what I needed. After some time, I realized that it isn't about trying to be the big dog. It's really just about being the best version of yourself that you can be. By keeping that in mind, I was able to work toward something attainable that would provide me what I needed and wanted. I kept trying different things until one success gave way to another, and then gave way to another. It is this willingness to try repeatedly that made me succeed where others often fail.

You must understand and know what motivates you when you are struggling or looking for solutions to improve your life. It takes a great deal of sacrifice and work to get what you want, and you're not going to reach any of your goals if you aren't motivated and don't remain motivated. That's why it's important to focus on what awaits you at the end of your road to financial freedom.

Security

The first and most obvious benefit of turning your life around and gaining that highly sought-after financial freedom is security. Security can mean different things to people. It may mean monetary security or emotional security or both. It's true that having a healthy savings account can really help you sleep at night and once you get a taste of that good feeling, you want more of it. You can see how one accomplishment leads to another. Knowing that you're going to be fine even if a costly emergency arises has a priceless calming effect on even the most neurotic of people. In this sense, financial security has also given you peace of mind.

Financial security for me meant being able to live comfortably from day-to-day while also ensuring that same level of comfort later in life. This meant contributing to an investment account that would allow for fun and travel. This didn't happen all at once, but was a gradual accumulation of funds over time. Few people realize that with investments, time works for you more than large amounts of money. If you start when you are young, it takes a very small amount over time to make you a millionaire. The trouble is that few people are consistent so they constantly live in a state of financial chaos and insecurity waiting for the next crisis.

For example, if you're like most people, you have one vehicle that you drive on a daily basis. Have you ever started that vehicle up in the morning or been sitting a traffic light when you hear an unfamiliar and alarming noise coming from the engine compartment? You can feel a tinge of worry shoot through your body as you envision a week without your only means of transportation. You envision a bill from your mechanic somewhere north of $700.00. A mechanical problem with your car, even a minor one, can snowball into a major headache. But for those with the financial reserves to deal with such a problem easily, a malfunctioning car is just a slight hassle—nothing more than a minor inconvenience in our lives. That's the kind of worry-free life that awaits you if you choose.

The vast majority of people that I've been around say they would love to travel and traveling abroad is one of the best ways to enrich your life and expand your horizons. Not only that, but it's fun to vacation on sunny beaches and learn about different people. That's one of the things I love about my new, financially secure life, and it's what you have to look forward to if you embark on and continue your journey. You will get to experience vastly different landscapes and cultures that will show that there is truly more to life than your worn, routine path. I got my first taste of this traveling to Miami with my children. While you may not consider Miami, Florida "abroad," it was for me and was one of the few trips I was able to justify because they were for a business purpose as well as for enjoyment. We also went on a 7 day cruise. My kids and I had an amazing adventure, they had so much freedom on the ship, saw so many new places and cultures. We bonded as a family and my eldest helped a great deal as we made our journey from Miami back home by car, with me as the only driver. It was a lot of fun and it was so awesome that we still talk about it to this day with fondness. I believe this is one of the reasons my kids today have such a joy of travel and travel a great deal.

It may surprise you to know that a very small percentage of people ever travel more than a few hundred miles from home – and many of those that have had some sort of overseas travel only did so in the military! A recent statistic I saw from the French government was that 75% of their population never traveled outside of France. Of course, they were saying this was positive confirmation that they had so much to offer that their citizens didn't need to go anywhere but I think it's a little sad. By comparison to Canada or the US, France is a small geographical area which is bordered by, or within a short distance from some of the greatest European cultures. I think this verifies how habitual we all are. We stay close to the places and people we are familiar with. Being comfortable with your surroundings is not necessarily a problem, but it can keep you from moving forward if others in your life are constantly critical or skeptical of your progress. As long as you are aware of this 'comfort zone' and commit to allowing yourself to experience new and different things on occasion, you can still succeed. I feel very fortunate that due to following my dreams and keeping my mind set on my goals, I was able to travel to many countries in the world including France, England and Italy among others.

The world is out there for you to see and enjoy, and turning your life around will make it available to you. But travel isn't the only change your lifestyle will see. You will find more leisure time to do the things that you enjoy. You can pursue other business opportunities without the stress of knowing that they absolutely must work out or you're sunk. You will have the opportunity to improve other areas of your life, like getting in shape and spending your free time doing things you truly enjoy rather than absorbing yourself in television or computer games because it's cheap entertainment. Your life has the potential to change dramatically for the better if you can see things through.

Time

If there's one thing I've learned through business, it's that relationships are key. When you find that you're able to slow down and enjoy your life, you'll realize how important all relationships are. And now that you have time to do what you want to do, you can spend time developing those relationships. Of course, no relationships are as rewarding as those you have with your family. Now you have time to spend back home with your parents without worrying about taking time off of work . You can go on vacation with your kids without always adding up the final cost of it in relation to your missed income in your head. You can, for lack of a better term, afford to stop constantly thinking about money and just enjoy having downtime and more of it.

I don't need to go into the importance of time with family because we all know how much we need those people in our lives, even if we have strained relationships at times. With your newfound freedom, there will be more of that time to spend with those who are most important to you. And the great thing about spending time with your family is that it can never be taken away. No matter what happens down the road, you will always have the time you spent with your family, and that is truly invaluable. When your journey is at an end and you look back on your life, you probably won't think, "I should have worked more overtime and skipped some family time."

Few of you would argue that friendships enrich our lives and having more time to spend with others will allow you to develop those friendships to the fullest. That stands to benefit you in a number of ways. Strong social networks have the power to make us healthier and happier both mentally and physically. After as you begin to change your life, you will have the time and energy to invest in those around you to produce some satisfying and strong bonds with the people you love. We all have a natural need for friendship. Friends can make all the difference in the human experience if you will just let them.

I've also found more than enough time to pursue my other interests. You may enjoy classic cars, traveling, reading, gardening or a million other things, and you will have the time to enjoy them. For me, I really enjoy what I do. I love my work and relieving the financial stress in my life has allowed me some room to play in the business world. I can make some riskier investments, follow my desires wherever they lead me and I cannot put a price tag on that. I have a passion for fitness, so I swim and do weights. I also take the time to eat right.

I met an older man by the name of Philip who, in the twilight of his life, was writing books and having a wonderful time doing it. He had worked hard his entire life and it wasn't until his retirement that he was able to pursue his real interest. While it was good to see him enjoying what he's doing now, I thought it was a shame that he had to wait so long to start. There was no reason that Philip couldn't have started writing 20 or 30 years sooner, but he never figured out that he could do what he wanted sooner with some life changes. Don't count on 'someday' to do those things you dream of as someday may not be there as you'd hoped.

Self-Esteem

There's no ego boost on the planet quite like having a hefty bank account, financial security and the freedom to do what you like, and that's what awaits you. Getting your finances in order and gaining that financial freedom will fill you with a sense of accomplishment that is almost unmatched by anything else you can do in life – at least that's been my experience. Turning my life around has totally changed my personality from a pessimist seeking escape to a happy and confident person. I owe a great deal of that to my successes in business and how I drastically changed an unhealthy lifestyle for the better. My personal experience has been that my friends and family were of the upmost importance and kept me going many times when I felt weak.

When you have successfully met all of your goals, you will experience this same rise in self-esteem. You will be able to take great satisfaction in knowing that you did such a wonderful job – in short you will feel proud of yourself and hold your head high - and it is a wonderful thing. You changed your life for the better, and that has an effect on all the lives around you. Your spouse, if you have one, will likely feel more happy and secure. Your children too. You will be happier, healthier and someone people enjoy being around. You can puff out your chest knowing that you've come farther and faster than anyone could have imagined – even you!

I also like to relieve stress and just let go by getting on the water on one of my extremely fast jet skis and jump some waves from cabin cruisers going by. Taking a long leisurely boat ride also gives me time to reflect and be grateful for this wonderful life that I have. Many of these moments are spent with the people that I love and care about, but most of these moments would not have been possible without their support and encouragement to carry on and not quit short of my goals.

You will see a change in the way your family looks at you, also. You will have gone from someone that they can't count on to pay the electric bill every month to their rock of financial strength and advice. They will know that they can count on you for anything – that you're the one to turn to when things go wrong. That is an incredibly satisfying feeling. When your family depends on you, it really puts a smile on your face and gives you the confidence to do anything and confidence is a very attractive quality. Have you ever noticed someone who walked into a room with a smile? It's because they command attention. They are confident and happy, and those are qualities worth noticing. And not only are you more noticeable with a smile, but the opinions of those noticing can be quite flattering. I'm often judged to be about 40 years old despite being in my 50s. I chalk it up to my perpetual smile – though maybe it has just as much to do with my full head of hair and using some of my available me-time to stay relatively physically fit. The benefits can be so much more than financial. Life has expanded and opened up in so many ways I didn't even expect.

Earned self-esteem is a term used to describe a positive self-image attained by first accomplishing something significant. That is what you are doing when you decide to take control of your life. You are gaining self-esteem in what I feel is the most respectable way. Like the term says, you are *earning* the confidence in yourself to do what you want to do and that is a lasting kind of confidence.

Giving Back

Charity, tithing, donating, giving back, paying it forward – call it whatever you want, but you will have the ability to do it soon. And you should. There are few things that are as rewarding as giving, and you will be in such a wonderful position to do so on a meaningful level. Not to undervalue those that give an occasional afternoon to a soup kitchen or a few boxes of used clothes to their local Salvation Army, you can do all these things as well. But there is much more to do and with some financial help, many of these organizations can have the flexibility to do some of the things that take money.

Of course there are many was to give back and you can start where you are now – you don't have to wait. Sharing your knowledge with others who have the same goals that you have is a great way to give your time and knowledge. We already covered in an earlier chapter the importance of a mentor, and that's essentially what you would be for someone else. There are a lot of people out there who will tell you how rewarding it is to mentor, though they may refer to it as coaching. It's a popular term these days, and just about everyone is willing to do it… for a price. Try some pro bono coaching/mentoring and see how rewarding it feels.

Another way to lead others is to teach. Teaching may not pay well, but ask anyone who's good at it and they will tell you how good it feels to help others gain knowledge and realize their full potential. Whether you teach children or adults, whether formally or in some kind of coaching program, teaching is much the same as mentoring and gives you the same feeling of worth and importance.

Experiments have been conducted to examine "luck" in peoples' lives. One such study asked people to count the number of pictures in a sample newspaper. The researcher conducting the study noticed that those people who described themselves as lucky were more likely to see a half-page ad on the second page of the newspaper that discretely read, "Stop reading – there are 43 photographs." Those who considered themselves unlucky discovered the ad with less frequency. The study was meant to prove that you make your own luck in life. I find that the harder and more focused I work, the luckier I get.

I'm sure that at some point, you will discover that you make your own luck in life. If you believe in yourself, even when you experience failures, you will keep moving forward toward your goal because you believe a positive outcome is approaching. Then you will have the opportunity to let others in on that secret. When you get through to them, and some will be more difficult than others, it can be incredibly gratifying to see them believe in themselves and know that you are part of the reason they do.

When you can help someone realize that luck is merely something that follows opportunities and the more attempts you make, the greater your "luck" in the end proves to be, the more rewarded you will feel.

But don't discount the importance of giving monetarily. Have you ever heard that what you put out comes back to you? It applies to a lot of things, from your outlook to your bank account. Giving money away with no expectation of getting any in return by itself will provide a gratifying feeling. But in many cases, if you send money out, you eventually receive that money back in one form or another. In fact, when you give without any selfish expectation, you will receive back many times over.

If you think that giving money away has nothing to do with getting money in return, it's time to change your thinking. The two actually intertwined. The more money you bring in, the more you should give away. It doesn't matter who it goes to. Give it to whoever made you happy, made you feel uplifted, helped you turn your life around – or to your source of spiritual renewal. And don't give grudgingly, expecting an immediate return. This is not an investment opportunity; you are giving. Give freely and become the vessel through which money passes.

We are what money flows into and out of. When you hoard money, you choke off the flow from one person to the next. Give the money away, keep the flow moving, and enjoy the ride. You've heard that it's much harder to get something moving than it is to keep it moving, and you need to apply that principle to money. Keep it flowing by giving it away rather than stopping the flow. The feeling is satisfying beyond anything I can describe. I have had the privilege to be of help on a number of occasions and it has enriched my life more than I would have believed.

Find Your Reason

I believe that motivation is the single most important part of your journey. Without the proper motivation, you will never accomplish what you set out to do. Any goal worth achieving is going to require you to sacrifice, work hard and struggle through some tough times. If you're doing all of those things for the wrong reasons, your chance of making it through are at more of a disadvantage than you might think.

Everyone is different and everyone can be motivated in different ways. For some, being a shining example of a good person to their new child may be reason enough in itself to turn your life around and do what you always wanted to do. Still others may be motivated by the chance to make large sums of money or travel or have a lot of free time. What drives you will likely differ from what drives others, and it's vital to discover what motivates you. Without the true reason you are doing the things you're doing and a pure and clear understanding of the reason you are doing it, you're going to need more luck than you are likely to find.

I can suggest the possibility riches beyond your wildest dreams until I'm blue in the face, but if you are not motivated by money or some other dream or right reason, you will never start the process of changing your life. It is absolutely necessary to find what motivates you to get up, sacrifice, work every day, and struggle to find what works for you until you have accomplished your goals. Find your reason and make a beginning (no matter how small).

At the beginning of this book, I talked about making a decision to change – that's the first step. But I'm reminded of the story of three frogs on a log. The three frogs are sitting on a log by a stream, catching the occasional bug that floats by. This is where they were born and what they know of life, yet the stream winds a great distance and they can see that far away is a beautiful lake. They've talked about going to the lake and imagined what it might be like, but here they still sit on the log. So one day one of the frogs makes the decision to go downstream and see what the lake is like. Now how many frogs are left on the log?

Most people would say two – but they would be incorrect. There are still three frogs. One made a decision to change, but without action that decision is not much good. How many times in the past have you made a decision to change only to have it fall by the wayside? Action is key to progress and so you must start your journey with the first step and keep on moving.

One of the first actions you must take is to set good goals. These give you direction and allow you to measure your progress. As each small goal is accomplished toward your big goal, a sense of accomplishment will appear that keeps you going even through the hard times. And there will be hard times – when you have a setback, make a mistake, or experience some unforeseen traumatic event. It is how you responded to these occasions that determines whether you will continue to move forward or be stopped in your tracks. Your *Altitude* can be boundless but it is totally affected by your *Attitude*. Mistakes will happen; shake them off and move on. I had many, many setbacks and at times felt like it was just too hard. It was at those times my friends, family and my reason kept me going. You can keep going as long as it takes!

Years ago, someone believed in me much more than I believed in myself. People such as this are invaluable and provide that emotional support when you may be unsure of yourself or unsure of your path. I encourage you to create good relationships with those who will support you and help you find your way to success. There are more of these people in your life right now than you know. Seek them out and you will have the support and advice that will carry you through. I certainly found this to be true for me. My work is far from done; I have many family members and friends I hope will follow some of the suggestions in this book. Changing my life also changed me in so many positive ways and what you become on your journey stays with you, so why not become better, smarter, more informed and wealthier with a more positive outlook? It can only help and who knows where you will end up.

Your path will be different from mine, but I hope that something I have conveyed in this book helps you along the way. Millionaires come in all shapes and sizes these days and it's not as hard to achieve as you might believe. I have learned it's not about the money; that will happen if you are pursuing your dreams. It's about the relationships you form with people. Allow yourself to learn from them and enjoy your time together. Making lots of money is not as hard as you think, and not as easy as I make it sound. It takes some work and motivation, but if I can do it – an alcoholic, mixed up punk without much to offer – than anyone can. There's no reason to think that you or someone else does not have the ability to succeed. I would encourage you to stop making excuses and take control of your own destiny. No one can do it for you nor should they. The future is yours to create and you choose what that future looks like starting today. So dream big about wealth, travel, fine dining, nice cars, a big house or that cottage escape. Whatever it is, it's not out of your reach if you just remember that there will be setbacks and you can overcome them.

Quitting is simply not an option!

Good luck and good health on your journey.